MYSTERIOUS TALES
OF THE
North Carolina Piedmont

MYSTERIOUS TALES
OF THE
North Carolina Piedmont

SHERMAN CARMICHAEL | Illustrations by Josh Adams

THE
History
PRESS

Published by The History Press
Charleston, SC
www.historypress.com

Copyright © 2019 by Sherman Carmichael
All rights reserved

All illustrations by Josh Adams

First published 2019

Manufactured in the United States

ISBN 9781467144063

Library of Congress Control Number: 2019939738

This book is dedicated to Beverly Carmichael, who spent many hours correcting my mistakes; Ric Carmichael; Tamara Carmichael; Blake Mahaffey; Sean Mahaffey; my attorney, Greg Askins; Cindy James; and Lynette Goodwin.

Contents

CONTENTS

CONTENTS

Just a Thought

L et's examine a few things. First let's ask the question, what are ghosts? Are they really the spirits of the dearly departed that didn't cross over for some reason? Are they hanging around to watch over their loved ones or their property? Are the spirits trapped somewhere in between here and there?

There is a confusing mixture of tabloid television, poorly researched sightings and, worst of all, hoax videotapes and pictures trying to convince us that they have caught a spirit on film. Our minds have been polluted by the unprofessional distortion of the data.

First, some ghosts can be explained as the result of an overly active imagination. For instance, if you have been preconditioned that a house, a graveyard or any other place is haunted, you will imagine that you hear and see or actually hear and see things and assume that it's a ghost, when in reality, it is nothing out of the ordinary.

Let's examine a few things that ghost hunters like to contribute to ghostly activity, the first being flickering lights. If you had a power meter on the power line to the light that's flickering, you would probably find that there is a slight power fluctuation, which will cause lights to flicker. Ghost orbs are popular with ghost hunters. Are orbs or floating spherical lights that are sometimes referred to as ghost orbs that are captured on film really ghosts? These have never been proven to have any connection with ghosts. They could be anything, including lens flare, bugs or dust particles reflecting light back into the lens. While you can't see it in person, it can be caught on film. I've been a photographer for thirty years and have had many pictures come out with so-called ghost orbs. None of my photos was taken in haunted places.

At locations of an alleged haunting, when you pick up a cold spot or get a variation of the electromagnetic field or you think you see a shadow out of the corner of your eye, how do you know it's a ghost? With all the electronic equipment and cameras you can haul into a place, you still can't prove there's a ghost there. If we look at the recent history of the way we look and think, we're going up and down, back and forth—never forward. Many rely on machines and electronic items that have no scientific proof that they work.

Since nobody knows what kind of energy, if any, a ghost produces, how do we know that an unproven instrument is picking up a ghost? It might be picking up some form of energy not related to ghosts but from millions of miles away. Is a ghost simply an energy imprint of the person that has passed away?

Let's screen out the obvious misidentifications and see what is left. Let's replace obsolete thoughts and methods of finding ghosts with new ideas and methods. The old ones are not working. All these years and we still haven't proven there are ghosts. There's no way to scientifically study ghosts, so how do you prove their existence?

Now here's some food for thought. How do we explain hearing noises and then, when you check it out, finding that there's nothing there? An example of this is hearing dishes falling and breaking in the kitchen. When you get there, nothing has happened. Another example is the sound of gunfire on an empty battlefield. Where does the sound come from?

What are the images that we see that suddenly or gradually materialize over a period of seconds? How do people see a battle being fought on a battlefield that hasn't had a battle fought there for over a hundred years? Are these things ghostly images, or are you seeing a glimpse from the past? Why do these images and sounds keep appearing from the dim corridors of the past for no apparent reason? Do the souls of the dearly departed endlessly relive their former lives or certain events? Do the historical scenes that appear to some people coexist with us in our time? Could it be a time loop where a person relives the same event throughout eternity, and only a person at the right time and place can see it happening? Is death the final frontier?

Ghost stories have been around for as long as mankind has been telling tales. For stories to last that long, there must be a modicum of truth to them. Ghosts, spirits or whatever you want to call them are out there. Too many people have seen something. There is only one road that leads to the truth, and we haven't found it yet. Where there's an inquiring mind, there will always be a new frontier.

Did the Devil Visit North Carolina?

D id the devil take up temporary residence in North Carolina or just drop in for a visit? Why did Indians and early explorers give the names that they did to certain locations? Why were so many locations linked to the devil? Does the devil have a favorite place, or does he just pick a place and drop in for a visit? Are the names of these places just coincidence? Let's examine a few of the locations in North Carolina named after the devil himself.

DEVIL'S TRAMPING GROUND

Western North Carolina is home to one of North Carolina's most baffling places, the Devil's Tramping Ground. It is located in a wooded area about ten miles from Siler City near Harpers Crossroads, and it is one of the strangest places on the Eastern Seaboard. It is on private property that has been in Bob Dowd's family for over one hundred years. In recent years, campers have visited the place, leaving behind beer bottles, cigarette butts and other trash, along with graffiti and campfire remains. Therefore, permission must be granted before you can visit the site.

The Devil's Tramping Ground is not a recent addition to North Carolina. The site was discovered by settlers who came to the area before the 1800s and gave it the name. The legend goes that the devil himself visited this spot, calling up his demons to do his evil deeds while he paced around and around. The devil's pacing left a well-worn path in almost a perfect circle about forty feet in diameter. No plants will grow within the forty-foot circle. The surrounding vegetation grows up to the edge and then stops. The outside vegetation is perfectly healthy. Was the devil using this spot to plot some evil deed for mankind?

When people place objects inside the circle and return the next morning to check them, the objects have been moved to the outside of the circle or are unexplainably missing. Animals do not venture into the circle either; woodland creatures seem to shy away from the Devil's Tramping Ground. Hunters say that when they're hunting in the area, their hunting dogs refuse to go into the circle. The needle spins wildly when you place a compass inside the circle.

There are a lot of theories about the Devil's Tramping Ground. Some people have suggested that the ground is sterile. The cause of the sterile land has been suggested to be everything from the result of a UFO landing or ancient crop circles to sacred burial grounds, possessed land and radiation. Another theory is that it was the site of an animal-powered gristmill or a location for Indian gatherings.

Tests have been run on the soil inside the circle and have revealed a high content of salt. Where did the salt come from, and why is it only in this small circle? In 1954, the state ran soil tests on samples from the circle. The results showed the ground was sterile, probably from the high concentration of salt. Scientists from the United States Geological Survey have visited the place but cannot find a reason for the lack of vegetation. Scientists and other researchers have examined the Devil's Tramping Ground only to offer no explanation why plants won't grow in the circle.

Richard Hayes, a thirty-year North Carolina soil scientist, tested the circle. He found no copper or high concentration of salt. There was nothing in his results in a high enough quantity to inhibit growth. Hayes retested the soil in September 2015. The results were sent to the state lab for a new analysis. The results suggested that vegetation should be growing. The soil inside the circle is no less fertile than the area outside the circle.

Job chapter 2, verse 2: "And the Lord said to Satan, 'From where do you come?' So Satan answered the Lord and said, 'From going to and fro on the earth, and walking back and forth on it.'"

DEVIL'S FOOTPRINT

Located in Largo, North Carolina, in Warren County off State Road 1131 is one of the most unexplained mysteries in the Tar Heel State. Many stories tell how the devil must have visited North Carolina, and some believe this confirms it. The devil left his footprint in a large stone known as the Devil's Rock. The footprint—at twelve inches long and one inch deep—is slightly larger than that of a human and is imprinted deep into the rock. The print is of the left foot. The rock is thirty feet long and fifteen feet wide.

One source says this story started in South Carolina. The devil's matching right footprint can be found in Flat Rock, Lancaster County, South Carolina. Sometime during the last century, a man lived in Flat Rock. He was said to be the meanest man to ever walk the face of the earth. He spent every minute he could doing nasty things. As the man grew older, knowing his time was running out and expecting to meet his maker anytime, he knew where he was headed. He didn't want to go there, but getting to the promised land didn't look too good. The crotchety old cuss devised a plan when he realized his time was drawing near. He bought a bunch of sharp tacks and placed them on the rock from which Flat Rock gets its name. He covered the tacks with old leaves and sat down to wait on the devil to arrive. Just as he expected, the devil appeared before him, ready to carry his soul away.

The devil asked, "Are you ready?" The old man replied, "I am, but I'd like to get a good look at you before we go. When I'm down there, I won't get a chance to see what you look like. If you please, would you kindly back up a little bit so I can get a full view of you?"

The devil stepped back and stepped right on the tacks. He jumped into the air, pushing down so hard that he left his footprint in South Carolina. The devil went up so high that he landed miles away in North Carolina. He came down with such an impact that his left foot was forced into the rock, leaving his footprint.

The devil was too scared to have the old man in the fiery pits of hell, and the man was so mean that heaven didn't want him either. The legend says that the ghost of the man who outwitted the devil walks the land between the two footprints.

The rock is still there, but the Department of Transportation reduced its glory when it dynamited the Devil's Rock to build a new road. The rock is on private property, so get permission before you venture out there.

DEVIL'S CAVE

There are legends across America about well-hidden caves where the Prince of Darkness lives. These stories have been handed down from the Indians to the white man over the past couple hundred years or so. Here's one from Richmond Hill in Yadkin County, North Carolina.

At the backside of an abandoned quarry is a cave where the Indians believed a powerful spirit lived. To reach it, you have to travel down a long dirt road to the quarry. Some of the locals believe that the cave is home to

The Devil's Cave

none other than the devil himself. For many years, visitors to the cave could hear sounds coming from inside the cave that sounded like groans.

Sometime between the late nineteenth and early twentieth century, four boys decided to journey into the cave and do a little investigating. Armed with a couple of lanterns and a few items gathered up from their homes to use as weapons, they headed to the cave. When they arrived, they noticed that all the normal noise from the woods had gone quiet. Not even the Yadkin River could be heard.

When they entered the cave, everything they said echoed back. One of the boys yelled into the cave, "Come on out here, devil," but there was no echo. They reported hearing noises coming from outside the cave that sounded like hoofbeats rather than footsteps. They dropped their lanterns and makeshift weapons and made a strategic withdrawal back to the safety of their homes. The legend says that the boys' hair had turned white by the next day.

THE HAUNTED WOODS OR THE DEVIL'S GUT

These haunted woods are located on Highway 64 between the county seat of Williamston and Jamesville in Martin County, North Carolina. From the earliest times to the present, strange and mysterious things have been happening here. Whether these woods are cursed or just fortunate to have so many strange things going on inside their boundaries is a mystery.

This stretch of swampland is home to mysterious small balls of light. For years, hunters have shot at them, scientists have studied them and they have been seen by many people. Attempts to capture the lights have failed miserably.

Many believe the lights are the souls of the early settlers who were massacred by the Indians near Roanoke River. Unable to rest, the souls just fly around the swamp.

Scientists' feeble attempts to give an answer as to what these balls of light are have not satisfied the local residents. The scientists' explanations are swamp gas, hunters' lights or headlights from cars.

Mysterious things other than balls of light have appeared in the woods. The ghosts of humans and animals have made an appearance. Stories of white deer, white cows and white dogs have come out of the haunted woods. These animals don't seem to be affected by hunters' bullets.

Another mystery is the hanging tree or lynching tree, an especially haunted area. The story behind this is that a man accused of being a horse thief could not prove his innocence and was hanged from a limb on that tree. People started seeing the full form of a man hanging from the same limb that the horse thief was hanged from. Some say the figure is opaque, while others describe it as giving off a pale silvery glow.

Due to the huge amount of violence and lost souls wandering in the woods, some refer to it as the Devil's Gut.

The Catsburg Ghost Train

I found several references to the Catsburg ghost train on the Internet. It seems that an abandoned railroad track runs close to the Catsburg Country Store. The store was closed and abandoned in the 1980s. Every so often, usually on moonless nights, a strange and mysterious light appears on the tracks down from the Catsburg Country Store. It looks like the light from an oncoming train. When the light appears, you can hear the sound of a train engine and the train whistle. The light never seems to move.

The Catsburg Ghost Train

It remains there for several minutes or less and then just fades into the darkness.

Some say you can see the headless ghost of the man who lost his life to a train while walking down the tracks. The accident that took the man's life seems to be replaying itself. Whether you get to see the ghost or not, it's well worth the trip to see part of the area's history before it's gone forever.

The Catsburg Country Store was built in the 1920s by Sheriff Eugene "Cat" Belvin on Old Oxford Road in the north end of Durham County. The store became an early landmark due to its high front façade and the image of the black cat above the name. For years, the Catsburg Country Store was the gathering place for the locals whom Eugene Belvin served as sheriff from 1928 to 1958. The Belvin family owned the Catsburg Country Store until it closed.

The information I found says it is now owned by M.M. Fowler and is on private property. Get permission before you visit.

1891 Bostian's Bridge Train Derailment

The Train Wreck that Started the "Ghost Train" Legend

The *Landmark Statesville* newspaper article read, "The most horrible disaster in the history of the railroad in North Carolina occurred at 2 o' clock in the morning at Bostian's Bridge over Third Creek two miles west of Statesville."

On August 27, 1891, the westbound passenger train number 9 passed Statesville at 1:52 a.m. on the Western North Carolina track headed for Asheville, North Carolina. The passenger train was known as the "Fast Mail." The train was composed of baggage cars, a mail car and first- and second-class coaches. The train also contained a Pullman sleeper car, the Saluda, and Superintendent R.R. Bridges's private car, Daisy.

At 2:00 a.m., train number 9 jumped the track on Bostian's Bridge and plunged sixty feet into the darkness below. Part of the train landed in Third Creek, damming the creek. The train was traveling between twenty-five and thirty-five miles per hour.

Bostian's Bridge, frequently referred to as Bostian Bridge, was constructed of brick and granite. It was built in 1857 and stands slightly over sixty feet high at its highest point.

The engine struck first, killing engineer William "Uncle Billy" West and fireman Warren E. Frye. Several cars landed on top of the other cars, trapping people inside. The survivors of the crash found themselves with another problem: the water was rising.

Passengers who were able made their way back to the train depot to get help and warn other trains that the track was out. No one in the sleeper car

survived the crash. Some of the injured passengers who were able climbed on top of the cars to escape the rising water and wait for help to arrive.

Colonel Benneham Cameron, a passenger on the ill-fated train, rescued a few of the passengers before going to Statesville for help. He borrowed a horse and buggy from local resident Gilbert Caldwell and made his way to town to gather up some volunteers. George Bowley of the Atlantic Rubber Company also made his way to town to get help.

Citizens in vehicles and on foot hurried to the scene of the tragic accident. Those who got there first encountered a harrowing spectacle.

Statesville had no hospitals, ambulances, rescue personnel or morgue. There were five doctors living in the area. The more seriously injured were taken to the homes of nearby residents and were taken in by families. The less injured were taken by buggy or wagon to town and put up in hotels. Those who went on to meet their maker were taken to a tobacco warehouse. Twenty-two people lost their lives in the accident.

There are two different stories about baggage master Hugh K. Leinster (also spelled Linster). Story one is that on August 26, he had received his gold watch for thirty years' service and was looking forward to his retirement. He never made it to retirement. He was killed on impact.

Story two is that Hugh K. Leinster was twenty-four years old and was killed by a falling trunk during the wreck. He was recently engaged to a young lady from Salisbury, North Carolina; he had grown up in Statesville. Leinster was laid to rest on August 28, 1891.

The Ghost Train

With all ghost stories, there are conflicting times, dates and versions of the story. Perhaps this ghostly image is nothing but a reflection from the distant past. I have included this information as I have found it in several different sources. There has been a long history of ghost trains.

One year after the wreck, on August 27, 1892, a small group of people was walking near the bridge when they heard a loud sound as if a train had wrecked. On their way to get a closer look, they met a man wearing a railroad uniform. As they approached him, he asked them for the time. They gave him the time and continued on to where the sound had originated. There was nothing there. They hurried back to see the man. He tipped his hat to them and walked away, vanishing. One of the people in the group said he looked at the man's watch and it looked to be three o'clock.

On the fiftieth anniversary of the train wreck, on August 27, 1941, the Hayes family from Columbia was traveling through Statesville in the early morning. While traveling on Buffalo Shoals Road within viewing distance of the bridge, their car got a flat tire. With no tools in the car to change the tire, Larry Hayes left Pat and the children in the car while he went for help. Pat witnessed a train approaching. As she watched the train go onto the bridge, the lights suddenly left the bridge and went down as the train ran off the bridge. Hearing the sound of the train crashing, Pat ran to the scene. Just before she got there, she met a man in an old-fashioned railroad uniform. He asked her the time, and she replied a little after 3:00 a.m. The man and the train then disappeared.

Not a Ghost Train: The Death of a Paranormal Investigator

A twenty-nine-year-old paranormal investigator (name withheld) and a group of amateur ghost hunters were gathering about midway across the bridge trying to find some paranormal evidence at the site of the August 27, 1891 train wreck.

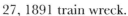

A train started approaching from the west. This was not a ghost train; this was a real train. The engineer spotted the ghost hunters as he rounded the bend. He blew the horn to warn the people on the bridge, but he was unable to stop the train in time. According to WBTV in Charlotte, the amateur ghost hunters were slow in responding because they thought it was a ghost train. Realizing it wasn't, they made a hurried attempt to get off the bridge. All but two made it. One victim, realizing that he and his girlfriend weren't going to make it, pushed her off the bridge. She suffered severe injuries from the fall but survived. The ghost hunter's body was thrown into the ravine from the impact of the train.

Ghost Lights

Ghost lights have been striking awe since first being witnessed. These orbs or balls of light normally seen at night can be seen with the naked eye if they are light-emitting. Some ghost hunters believe these lights to be the souls of the dearly departed who were the victims of deep tragedy or suicide and are destined to never find peace. Most lights can be explained relatively easily. Earth lights are believed to be produced by tectonic strain in earthquake faults. St. Elmo's fire is an electrical discharge often observed around ships. Fox fire is a naturally occurring phenomenon. Its source is a bioluminescent fungus growing in special conditions such as rotting wood. Will-o'-the-wisps are lights moving about over marshy ground. These are just a few examples of what some think are ghost lights. Most of what people are seeing is nothing more than a naturally occurring light. However, there are the few that can't seem to be categorized as natural phenomena. These balls of light are seen floating around or stationary and usually at a distance. Every state in the United States has reports of ghost lights. Now we're going to take a look at a few from North Carolina that are still baffling people and scientists. Generations of North Carolina natives have grown up hearing about the Brown Mountain Light and the Maco Light. Do these lights have an unearthly origin? Some defy explanation.

In a May 20, 2002 article in the *Winston-Salem Journal*, Dan Canton, a physics and astronomy professor at Appalachian State University, states that 90 percent of strange light can be attributed to man-made sources. The other 10 percent is interesting science such as atmospheric optics playing tricks.

MINTZ LIGHT

Five miles west of Roseboro is the small crossroads community of Mintz, located in Sampson County. There isn't much folklore documenting this light; it seems to be just another story of a railroad ghost light. I couldn't find any record of a death on the railroad connected to the Mintz Light. If it wasn't for the frequency of the ghost light sightings along the nearby railroad tracks in the early 1960s, no one would probably have ever heard of Mintz. The appearance of the Mintz ghost light became so routine that it became Mintz's only tourist attraction. Witnesses describe it as a small light moving around on the railroad tracks like an old lantern. I couldn't find anything saying whether the light can still be seen.

EPHRAIM'S LIGHT

There is not much documentation on Ephraim's Light. In North Hampton County near the town of Seaboard is a preserved plantation house called the Woodruff house, which dates back to the early 1800s. The Woodruff House is home to a ghost light, an eerie yellowish light that occasionally appears in the downstairs rooms and can be seen through the window. The light seems to move around from room to room before it vanishes.

The legend is that a slave named Ephraim is believed to have killed his owner, Martin Woodruff. After the murder, Ephraim escaped from the plantation. After the master's body was found, a posse was formed and soon tracked down Ephraim. They brought him back to the plantation to deal out the horrible plantation punishment. The posse burned Ephraim

at the stake. Soon after the death of Ephraim, the light began to appear.

The old-timers believe it's the restless spirit of Ephraim bound to the place where he met such a horrible death.

FREMONT LIGHT

There is not much information on this ghost light; I could find only one source on the internet. The legend of the Fremont Light is that a man in Fremont got so inebriated that he couldn't ride his horse home. He left the horse in Fremont and started walking home on the railroad tracks that run through the town. The story says that in his inebriated state, he didn't get off the railroad tracks in time, and officials later ended up peeling him off the front of the train. Down the tracks where the

accident happened, you can sometimes see a small red glow off in the distance kind of wobbling down the railroad tracks. The only reference to what the glow might be is the man's cigarette.

VANDER LIGHT

Vander is a small town in Cumberland County located between Fayetteville and Stedman, North Carolina. It lies at the junction of Interstate 95 and Clinton Road. It is famous for more than its friendly, laidback atmosphere. One of its residents, Archer Matthews, has become a legend—the man believed to be haunting the railroad tracks.

Like every ghost story, this one has several different versions. On a clear October evening, just before suppertime when the sun was sinking low, the switchman switched the railroad tracks for the next train's arrival. Out of the near darkness, the train appeared, barely slowing down for the crossing and knocking the man into its path. Naturally, the train cut off the switchman's head.

Another version is that on a clear night, the switchman was lost in thought and fell onto the tracks as the train roared by, cutting off his head.

Another story is that on a rainy night, ticket master Matthews was waiting on the late-night train. He stood up to get a good look down the tracks. As he was turning to

Vander Light

head back into the ticket office, he heard a strange sound coming from across the tracks. He picked up his lantern and went to investigate. He slipped and fell onto the tracks, hitting his head. Unconscious, he was unable to move off the tracks. By the time the engineer saw Matthews lying across the track, it was too late. The train decapitated Matthews.

Not long after Matthews's death, reports started coming from people who saw the mysterious light near Vander Station. The train station is no longer there, but Matthews still walks up and down the now deserted tracks between Vander and Stedman, swinging his lantern. No matter how far you walk, the light stays ahead of you. If you turn around, you might see the light behind you. The light has been seen since the 1800s. Does the Vander light belong to Archer Matthews's lantern?

Haunted Bridges

Haunted bridges are a staple of American ghost stories. It seems that every state has at least one well-known haunted bridge with a phantom hitchhiker. If you look really closely, you just might find a haunted bridge in every county. Every story has different versions depending on who's telling it. The one part that usually doesn't change is the young woman coming from a prom or dance who is killed in a car wreck. She is always seen standing by the side of the road (or sometimes a bridge) trying to hitch a ride home. She never makes it home. She always vanishes just as the driver pulls up to the house at the address that she has given the driver. Then it plays over again. Some of the stories have been around since the horse-and-buggy days. Will these girls ever make it home?

Haunted bridge stories can also tell of an accident, murder or suicide that leaves the victim still haunting the bridge.

MORPHEUS BRIDGE

According to the legend, a family of three was driving home when their car ran off the road into Little River. This accident was supposed to have happened in the 1940s. However, no record of the accident could be found. Depending on where you get the story or who you talk to, the father lived but the mother and daughter died in the accident. Another source says all in the car were killed.

Now for the ritual. By the way, the bridge is still in use and can be very dangerous. Some say if you stop your car on the bridge and turn it off, the ghost of a female will appear crying and try to get into your car. Some say it's the daughter, while others say it's the momma. Others say you can see lights under the water. The lights are believed to be the headlights of the car.

Another story is that the car crashed into the side of the bridge and the family was thrown out and fell into the river. If you park your car on the bridge on Halloween, your car will cut off. Then a woman will appear as if searching for her child. Another version of the story is that the daughter will appear, and it seems she is looking for her parents.

Sightings of orbs and strange lights are common around the bridge.

Morpheus Bridge is in Wake County, North Carolina.

SALLY'S BRIDGE

Not much information is available on this bridge. The bridge was previously unnamed but given the nickname by the locals. Sally's Bridge runs over Clark Creek on Cox Mill Road near Concord, North Carolina.

The story behind the haunting tells that one night a young mother,

Sally, was driving home in a rainstorm. The car was either swept off the road by a flash flood or a sudden gust of wind or she just accidentally ran off the road. Her car plunged into Clark Creek. Sally and her baby were thrown from the car when it hit the creek.

Sally searched for her baby, but it was gone—drowned in the creek. It is unclear how Sally died. Depending on the source of the story, Sally drowned searching for her baby or committed suicide over the loss of her baby or just wasted away grieving over her lost child.

Now her ghost haunts the bridge. If you stop your car on the bridge, you can sometimes hear the cries of a child and the screams from Sally. Some say Sally will knock on the window of the car pleading for your help with finding her baby.

PISGAH COVERED BRIDGE

The historic Pisgah Covered Bridge in Asheboro, Randolph County, is one of North Carolina's two remaining covered bridges. It was built in 1911 by J.J. Welch at a cost of about forty dollars. The bridge is fifty-four feet long and crosses the West Fork Branch of the Little River in the Uwharrie National Forest.

The Pisgah Covered Bridge is off the beaten path but easily accessible. There are no signs to direct you there after you leave the interstate. When you reach the bridge, there is a small gravel parking lot.

In 2003, the bridge was washed away during a massive flood, but it was rebuilt using 90 percent of the original materials. It now has a new shingle roof, but it has been desecrated by vandals who have defaced it with graffiti.

In the 1920s, there was a hanging on the bridge, and on certain nights, you can see the ghostly figure of a man hanging from the rafters. If you cross the bridge at night, you might find yourself face to face with a terrifying apparition.

The bridge is open to the public during daylight hours only, which makes nighttime ghost hunting impossible. Don't trespass and don't vandalize the bridge.

TEETERS BRIDGE

County Road 1132 between Mount Pleasant Road South and Barrier Georgeville Road has a single small bridge. The bridge is located in Cabarrus County. The locals know it as Teeters Bridge. It was named in honor of a farmer, John Teeter, who lived nearby. However, this isn't the original bridge. The original small wooden bridge was known for flooding. Today, it is a modern concrete bridge.

The story goes that a young mom and her baby were on their way home during a heavy rainstorm. With almost no visibility, she ran off the bridge into Dutch Buffalo Creek. She and the baby drowned.

Now for the strange part of the story. Apparently, there is a large stone with the name "Furr" cut into it near the bridge. When it rains, the stone bleeds. Other stories say that there are stones along the creek bed that bleed, too.

Screams have also been heard along the bridge, and a dark figure has been seen wandering on the bridge. Some people report a shadowy figure going under the bridge.

Another source says a little girl was brutally murdered near Teeters Bridge many years ago. The family placed a marker in remembrance of their daughter.

Could it be what the stone is made out of that causes water to look like blood?

SEVEN BRIDGES ROAD

This is an unusual story. If you drive NC 97 east from Rocky Mount to the small hamlet of Leggett, North Carolina, you will cross over seven bridges. Now turn around and backtrack, and you will pass over only six bridges.

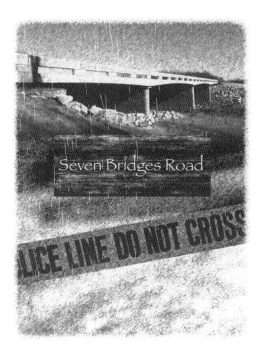

One bridge has vanished. Is it simply an optical illusion? Some believe there's a darker reason. Some believe the road is evil. Through the years, there have been a lot of accidents on this stretch of road. Several bodies were found next to the road.

There was supposed to be a serial killer suspected of killing ten women from Nash and Edgecombe Counties. Nine bodies were recovered; the tenth is still missing. Many of the women's bodies were found along Seven Bridges Road in the woods. There's not much information on the story.

LYDIA'S BRIDGE

In 1923, Lydia's prom night came to a tragic end. Lydia and her date were headed home from the prom when he lost control of the car on a sharp curve. Lydia's date was killed instantly.

Lydia managed to drag herself out of the crumpled car and into the pouring rain. Lydia suffered serious injuries, and in her blood-soaked prom gown, she died on the side of a lonely road trying to flag someone down. No one would stop and offer her assistance.

The locals were furious about the unnecessary deaths of two high school

Lydia's Bridge

students and demanded a bridge be built to prevent another accident on the curve. Just outside Jamestown, North Carolina, on Highway 70 is a bridge named in honor of Lydia. The bridge is no longer in use.

For over ninety years, people in Jamestown have reported seeing a lovely young woman—maybe seventeen or eighteen years old—in a white prom gown standing by the side of the road trying to flag someone down to take her home. If you are traveling along Highway 70 east of Jamestown near High Point and see Lydia standing by the roadside, give her a ride.

When the car pulls over to help the young woman, she will get into the back seat and introduce herself as Lydia. She tells the driver that she's been to the prom and is trying to get home. Lydia will tell the driver the address of her home, which is not too far away. As the driver drives off, he might try to engage Lydia in a conversation. She seems distracted and not interested in talking. The driver reaches the address and pulls into the driveway. He gets out of the car to open the door for Lydia only to discover Lydia's vanished.

The driver approaches the home and knocks on the door. An elderly lady answers the door. The driver tells the lady his story. The lady replies that she is Lydia's mother and that Lydia lived there until she was killed coming home from the prom. She shows the driver a picture, and he confirms that she is the young woman he picked up. The mother thanks the driver for picking up Lydia. The driver apologizes to the lady, graciously thanks her for her time and leaves.

There are a number of different versions to this and every other phantom hitchhiker story.

Many people have reported seeing Lydia by the side of the road. Many have claimed to have picked her up only to have her disappear. Some report that when passing under the overpass late at night, they have seen a young woman in the back seat of their car, only to have her vanish in a few seconds.

Now that the bridge is closed, you have to take U.S. 70A. Where it twists around a curve that passes by an old overgrown underpass, you might see a young woman standing on the side of the road trying to flag someone down.

On High Point Road from Greensboro heading toward Jamestown, there is an overpass at the "Welcome to Jamestown" sign. You can park nearby and walk through the thick vegetation to get to the old bridge.

What is the truth behind this story? I did locate some information that there exists a High Point (Guilford County) death certificate for Lydia Jane (last name withheld), born in 1904 in High Point, died on December 31, 1923, from fatal injuries sustained in a motoring accident. She would have been eighteen or nineteen at the time.

SCREAMING BRIDGE

The Screaming Bridge is located in Williamston, Martin County, near Little Washington on Yarrell Creek Road crossing the Sweet Water Creek.

One story about Screaming Bridge tells of a woman wearing a cat costume with red contacts. She was on her way from a Halloween party to pick up her baby. After she picked up the baby and continued toward her home, she ran off the bridge and into the river. You can still hear her screaming for her baby.

Another story connected to Screaming Bridge happened during the Civil War. A woman with the last name Yarrell was beaten by her husband and hanged herself from the bridge.

In another version of the story, the dead girl was Yarrell's daughter. For whatever reason, she mysteriously drowned in the river. Another variation is that she committed suicide in the creek. Her sister supposedly knew who killed her or why she was killed and ended up cutting her own wrist, ending her life on the bridge.

Whatever the true story, people began seeing and hearing the woman's ghost long before cars were around.

Another version of the story of Screaming Bridge is that if you sit on the bridge at midnight, you can see blood on the bridge where the woman killed herself or was murdered. Sometimes you can hear a woman scream off in the darkness.

Sometimes on moonless nights, the dead woman can be seen sitting on a cypress tree looking into the water. Some believe she accidentally drowned.

Screaming Bridge

Mount Pleasant Bleeding Tombstone

I couldn't find a lot of information on the bleeding tombstone. Most sources say a little girl was brutally murdered near Teeters Bridge, about fifty to seventy-five yards from where Miami Church Road connects with Barrier Georgevell in Mount Pleasant, Cabarrus County. One source says the family

buried the little girl near the bridge. Another source says the little girl was not buried there. The family erected a stone marker there in remembrance of their child. The story goes that when it rains, the stone bleeds a red-orange liquid.

Another version of the story is that a woman was swept away and drowned in her car during a big flood.

The marker has been vandalized, but part of it is still there.

Oakwood Cemetery

Oakwood Cemetery was established in 1869 by the Raleigh Cemetery Association. The cemetery is located in the historic Oakwood neighborhood of Raleigh on gently rolling hills adjacent to downtown. Both a Jewish and a Confederate cemetery lie in the boundaries of the Oakwood Cemetery. The Confederate cemetery contains 2,800 graves of Confederate soldiers who met with their untimely deaths in the Civil War. Today, historic Oakwood Cemetery's 102 acres are a beautiful resting place for the dearly departed. With its monuments and markers set off by oaks, cedars and flowering trees and a meandering stream, Oakwood stand out among other cemeteries.

A Confederate cemetery was established after the Civil War. A group of Raleigh women had an idea about a permanent burial place for the Confederate soldiers in 1866. The Confederate soldiers were laid to rest at the present Federal Cemetery on Rock Quarry Road. These dedicated ladies set out to find a final resting place for the fallen Confederate soldiers. Henry Mordecai donated the land the women needed to establish a cemetery. The ladies of Wake County began work on the new cemetery.

In 1867, a federal agent was sent to Raleigh to locate a site for a cemetery for Union soldiers. His location of choice was the Rock Quarry Cemetery. He gave the good citizens of Raleigh three days to move their Confederate soldiers. More than five hundred Confederate bodies were moved to the Mordecai property. The present Confederate Cemetery is cared for by the Sons of Confederate Veterans.

Oakwood Cemetery is known for being haunted. People say some of the spirits are quite angry, which is understandable. Visitors have reported being punched or receiving stings on their necks followed by red spots. Some have reported having their arms scratched.

Paranormal investigators report their flashlights stop working, and on nights when the temperature was in the seventies, their thermometers were reading cold spots of forty-seven degrees in some areas of the cemetery

Another legend of Oakwood Cemetery is the Spinning Angel. In the northwest corner of Oakwood is the statue of an angel often referred to as the guardian angel of Oakwood. The angel's head is supposed to spin around twelve times at midnight on every Halloween. Another legend involving the guardian angel tells that it will completely turn around if you watch it long enough at night. Others in the cemetery have said that the angel's eyes will follow your movements.

One source says that the angel is on the grave of Etta Rebecca White, who lived from 1880 to 1918. She passed away due to illness. Another source says the angel statue is of his grandmother Etta Ratcliff.

If they are still being offered, you can take a lantern walk through historic Oakwood Cemetery. This is not a ghost tour.

Gravity Hill

Nestled deep in the landscape of eastern Rowan County is an unusual place referred to as Gravity Hill. Gravity Hill is located a few miles down the road from Dan Nicholas Park on Richfield Road near High Rock Lake. Richfield Road looks just like any other country road except for the graffiti painted on it. Some people just have to vandalize something. Some believe that a place on this road defies the law of gravity.

Here's the story: stop your car at the bottom of Gravity Hill, put it in neutral, sit back and watch the car slowly move uphill. Some say you can put baby powder on the trunk of the car, and when your vehicle reaches the top of the hill, there will be handprints in the baby powder, as if someone or something was pushing the car uphill.

Like every other mystery, there are a number of stories giving different reasons for the car moving uphill under its own power or the power of something else. One night, a young mother and her daughter were driving on Richfield Road. The car stalled. The mother got out, leaving the child in the car while she was trying to push it uphill to safety. As she was nearing the top of the hill, an unsuspecting truck came along the dark road and, not seeing the car in time, hit it, killing the mother and child instantly. It seems that the mother is reliving that night again and again by pushing stalled cars up the hill.

Another account explains that a couple and their newborn baby were traveling on the road at the turn of the twenty-first century. The car turned over, crushing the child under it. The parents were able to crawl to safety, and they tried frantically to push the car off the child. Some believe that it's the parents pushing your car uphill still trying to push the car off their child.

Another version is that at the conclusion of the Civil War, some soldiers were returning to North Carolina and discovered an abandoned wagon full of crates. Thinking there might be food and supplies in the wagon, the soldiers pulled it until they found a place they considered safe. Before they could open the crates, they were attacked and killed by a group of Union carpetbaggers. When the Union carpetbaggers opened the crates, to their surprise they found them full of linen cloth. Now, the Confederate soldiers are returning to get their wagon uphill. Whichever story you believe is up to you.

There may be another explanation about Gravity Hill—a scientific one. There are those who believe in science and fact and there's a rational explanation. They claim that this is an optical illusion. While your eyes and senses have you convinced that you're going uphill, you're actually going downhill.

Sewer Monster

Is there another world in the ground beneath us? As we go about our business, is there an unknown creature lurking below us? Every city or small town has miles and miles of sewer pipes. What is lurking beneath us in these pipes? Sewer lines have long been the source of spooky tales and even a few B movies.

In April 2009, a South Carolina–based construction company was contacted to inspect the sewer lines beneath Cameron Village near Raleigh, North Carolina. The sewers were built in 1949. The company was checking for infrastructure problems and used surveillance cameras to inspect the sewer lines.

The camera came across something that no one was expecting: a slimy, pulsating blob attached to a sewer wall. It appeared to be a living organism of some unknown kind. The strange creature seemed to react to the camera light.

The video mysteriously popped up on YouTube before anyone took the time to try to find out what it was or if the video was real. It started picking up hits. It was dubbed the Cameron Village Sewer Blob.

NBC, FOX, ABC and many other news agencies started covering the story. With this kind of coverage, skeptics and believers came crawling out of the woodwork. Some believed it was extraterrestrial. Others believed it was a monster. Some believed it was an undiscovered animal, while others believed it was a mutant monster. The rumors ran wild. Then there were those who believed that the video was a hoax.

A spokesperson for the company confirmed the video was real, but she said that the colonies looked much larger on camera than they actually were.

Ed Buchan, a staff biologist for the Raleigh Public Utilities Department, confirmed the oddity was a colony of worms. A North Carolina State University biology professor thinks it's a colony of thousands of tiny organisms called bryozoans or moss animalcules. Dr. Timothy S. Wood, an expert on freshwater bryozoa and an officer with the International Bryozoology Association, said they are clumps of annelid worms, almost certainly tubificids.

There is no strange creature coming out of the sewers to devour the neighborhood or destroy all life on earth.

Unfortunately, most of the time there's a logical explanation to most mysteries if you take the time to look for it.

Lake Norman Monster

Throughout history, there have been sea monsters, river monsters and a few lake monsters. These creatures inhabit Loch Ness, Lake Champlain and Lake Okanagan, and let's not forget the Lake Murray Monster in South Carolina. The story of the Lake Murray Monster can be found in *Forgotten Tales of South Carolina*, by this author.

Whether these aquatic monsters are real or mythological, we may never know, unless one is captured or a dead one is found. We still get reports of sightings of lake monsters. The Piedmont area of North Carolina has its own lake monster. Over the years, hundreds if not thousands of people have reported seeing the Lake Norman Monster, affectionately called Normie.

Lake Norman is North Carolina's largest man-made lake. It was created between 1959 and 1964 by Duke Power Company. It took four years to build Cowans Ford Dam and two years to fill the lake. The lake is fed by the Catawba River. Lake Norman has 250 miles of shoreline. It is 34 miles long and 50 square miles. The deepest part is 130 feet at the Cowans Ford Dam—plenty deep to house a lake monster. The average depth of the lake is about 30 feet.

Two people on Lake Norman reported seeing a fish of some sort about thirty feet long that swam as fast as lightning. Another witness believed he saw a human-sized catfish. Another sighting described a long and serpent-like creature with strange-looking fins. Some have reported seeing it sunning on the shoreline. Another sighting was described as a crocodilian creature. There are reports of a three-humped serpent with a slender body with thick whisker-

like appendages, flippers and a dorsal fin. One person, while tubing on the lake, saw a large neck and head raise about five feet out of the water. Another report described the head as looking like a prehistoric dinosaur with a brown neck about ten feet long. People have reported seeing a creature about twenty feet long with a serpent body. Another report was a creature as big as a shark with an enormous black tail.

The most recent sighting was on January 22, 2007, by a man from Fox River, Illinois.

One theory about the Lake Norman Monster is that he is the result of a biological experiment that went wrong in which an Arkansas blue catfish was bred with a Wyoming buffalo carp, and the result was stocked in Lake Norman.

Science fiction has a way of becoming science fact. Is the Lake Norman Monster an atomic monster created by radiation exposure? The McGuire Nuclear station is located at the top of the lake. The McGuire Nuclear power plant went into operation in 1981.

A footnote to the story comes from the fact that a rare species of jellyfish was discovered living in Lake Norman in late 1990. The jellyfish is not indigenous to Lake Norman, and no one knows where they came from, how they got in the lake or how long they've been in there.

Carolina Butcher

Paleontologists from North Carolina State University and the North Carolina Museum of Natural Sciences discovered an unknown species while digging in the Pekin Formation in Chatham County, North Carolina. They recovered shattered parts of the prehistoric creature's skull, spine and upper forelimb. Due to the unique texture of the bones, it was identified as something new. Researchers determined that it belonged to a previously unknown species.

Because the skull was preserved in pieces, it was difficult to visualize what the complete skull looked like. Researchers scanned the skull bones with the latest imaging technology and created a three-dimensional model of the reconstructed skull. The sutures between the predator's skull bones weren't fused when the animal died, meaning this particular Carnufex was still growing when it started its 231-million-year journey into the fossil record.

The Pekin Formation contains sediments deposited 231 million years ago, in the beginning of the late Triassic period. At that time, North Carolina was a wet, warm equatorial region beginning to break apart from the super continent Pangea. This discovery predates dinosaurs.

The *Carnufex carolinensis*, or Carolina Butcher, was a nine-foot-long (at the time of death) land-dwelling crocodylomorph that walked in an upright position on its hind legs. It has a long skull that resembles a knife and blade-like teeth. It has a pronounced ornamentation of the skull. Its skull also has pits and grooves. It is one of the world's earliest and largest

crocodylomorphs, a group of creatures that includes modern and extinct crocodile relatives. The *Carnufex carolinensis* may have filled one of North America's top predator roles before the arrival of the dinosaurs.

The massive extinction at the end of the Triassic period killed off a large number of the world's big predators, including the large crocodylomorphs.

In the pages of *Scientific Reports*, paleontologists Lindsay Zanno, Susan Drymala, Sterling Nesbitt and Vincent Schneider threw back the curtain on the creature and confirmed that the rumors were true, according to *National Geographic*.

Guilford County Bigfoot

Two North Carolina men said they came upon two Bigfoot creatures in Guilford County. In January 2016, Coleman and his friend were looking for property to hunt on and decided to look at land in Oakridge. They arrived about 3:30 p.m. and followed the creek bed. They walked for about thirty minutes down the creek bank before finding a game trail and deciding to wait. After about a five-minute wait, they heard something moving in the nearby woods. It was making a lot of noise.

About forty yards away, the men saw something big crouched down by the creek. They started to get up when the animal they had been listening to in the woods stepped out of the woods onto the creek bank. The creature that came out of the woods walked over to the other one down by the creek, and then both walked away down the creek.

One of the creatures was bigger than the other. The creatures had shaggy brown hair with a little gray in certain areas. They had broad shoulders and massive arms and legs. The taller one was about eight feet tall and weighed over four hundred pounds.

Chupacabra

Since the legend of the mystical creature first emerged, there have been sightings of the Chupacabra all across the United States—or at least what people claim is a Chupacabra. As monster legends go, the Chupacabra is a fledging monster myth. It goes back about thirty to forty years in Mexico or Puerto Rico. Some say it appeared around 1970. Researchers are at a disagreement on what country had the mythical creature first.

The description of the Chupacabra differs from its origins to the present. One description has the animal about four to five feet tall, with long claws, red glowing eyes and spikes down its back. It has the ability to jump long distances. Some have it looking like a reptile creature with leathery, grayish skin and sharp spines down its back. It is three to four feet tall and hops similar to a kangaroo. Another recent description of the Chupacabra is that of a strange breed of wild dog. It is hairless and has a pronounced spinal ridge, pronounced eye sockets, fangs and claws. Others describe it as a demon straight from hell.

Others are convinced that it's just a normal animal like a fox, dog or some other known animal with the mange. DNA tests on some of the supposed Chupacabras have found them to be common mammals with parasitic infections causing their monstrous appearance. When the animals killed by a supposed Chupacabra are autopsied, they contain plenty of blood.

The Chupacabra leaves dead animals behind. Though goats are its favorite prey, it has been known to kill cats, rabbits, dogs and other animals.

Its victims are often drained of all blood from two to three holes like a vampire. The stories of the Chupacabra are quite conflicting.

Like any other strange thing, there are many theories about the origin of the Chupacabra. The most popular explanation is that it's a top-secret United States government genetics experiment gone bad. Other theories are that it's an extraterrestrial being. Some even think it's the wrath of God. Whatever it is, there's something here that's killing animals, and no one can positively say what it is.

The most recent sighting of the blood-sucking monster was in the Piedmont region of North Carolina. There have been other sightings across the Tar Heel State. There was no date or exact location given.

The name itself is derived from the Spanish *chupa* (to suck) and *cabra* (goat).

Giant Winged Creature

Pterosaurs were flying reptiles that existed during most of the Mesozoic period from the Triassic period up until the end of the Cretaceous period 228 to 66 million years ago.

Cynthia, a twenty-year-old female, has seen pterosaur-like creatures three times in Raleigh, North Carolina. She described the creature as dark brown and having a long tail with a diamond-shaped bulb on the end of it. Her latest sighting was at the North Raleigh bus stop on Thursday, January 4, 2018.

In Charlotte, a man and his cousin saw something bringing to mind a dragon. In Asheville, a lady saw a huge black winged creature that flew low over her car. In Jacksonville, North Carolina, a person saw something huge flying in the sky. It looked like it had a pale greenish-white skin. All accounts say the creature has smooth skin with no feathers and a long tail with a diamond shape at the end. A man was driving on Interstate 540 in Raleigh in late March 2013 when he saw a huge bird-looking thing fly across the overpass he was on. The creature was about twenty-five feet in front of him and about eight feet off the ground. Two witnesses saw a flying creature in 2007 on the south side of Raleigh. Another witness in Durham allegedly saw a pterodactyl in 1993. That creature had bat-like wings, and its wingspan was about ten to fifteen feet. Another eyewitness reported in 2010 that he saw something huge in the sky. It looked like it had pale greenish-white smooth skin and a long tail. It didn't appear to have any feathers.

Could these flying mystical beasts just be great blue herons? "While not absolutely impossible, living pterosaurs are highly unlikely," said Mat Cartmill, emeritus professor of evolutionary anthropology at Duke University.

For centuries, not one naturalist, explorer, farmer, hunter, trapper or biologist has run across a single specimen, living or dead.

North Carolina has long been home to legends of Bigfoot and the Lake Norman Monster. New sightings of flying pterosaurs have piqued the interests of local cryptozoologists. North Carolina is now considered by many cryptozoologists to be one of America's seven pterosaur hot spots.

Cryptozoology is a pseudo-science and subculture that aims to prove the existence of entities from the folklore record. Cryptozoologists are people who pursue animals that are undescribed and unsubstantiated by modern science yet are alleged to exist on a legend, hearsay or eyewitness sighting.

Mayodan Meteorite

In the 1920s, it was the responsibility of the county to maintain and repair the roads. Despite that, many times, neighbors would get together and repair the section of road that passed by their property.

James E. Beaver of High Point, Rockingham County, North Carolina, was working with a few neighbors in 1920 to repair a section of road in front of their property. They attempted to remove what they thought was another rock from the bank of the road. When they tried to move it, they found it was much heavier than a normal rock that size. When they finally got it moved, Beaver carried it home with him, where it remained for thirty years. He thought it was a meteorite from the start and often referred to it as a meteorite.

In September 1950, Beaver submitted a small fragment of the rock to the United States National Museum for identification. The sample proved that Beaver was right all the time—it was an iron meteorite. At the museum's request to see the main meteorite, Beaver sent it to them. When the museum received the meteorite, it weighed thirty-four pounds. It was an altered, irregular mass; none of the original flight surface was preserved. During the thirty years that Beaver owned the meteorite, it was stored inside part of the time and outside in the weather the rest of the time. The meteorite found by Beaver is a hexahedrite.

Sometime around 1890, a meteorite was seen and heard falling in that area. Several people reported the fiery object. Officials could not be sure if this was the same meteorite that was reported falling.

Monroe Meteorite

On Wednesday, October 31, 1849, at 3:00 p.m., a brecciated H4 chondrite meteorite fell in Cabarrus County, North Carolina. The recovered meteorite was the second witnessed fall in North Carolina since it became a state in 1789. It is the only one on record witnessed to have fallen in 1849 in the world.

Reports say that the earth-shaking impact left some nearby people with a near apocalyptic feeling. Some feared the end of the world was near

or the day of final judgment. Some people were surprised, and others were terrified by the sudden explosion, followed by two other explosions and a rumbling in the air.

On Monday, November 5, a servant of the Branch Mint of the United States in Charlotte brought a report from Cabarrus County that notices were stuck to trees inviting people to come see a rock that had fallen from the sky on Hiram Post's plantation. Post dug ten inches down to get to the rock.

Mr. Gibbon and Dr. Andrews traveled twenty-one miles to Hiram

Post's plantation to see the rock from space. There they found bluish, gritty rock about eight inches long, six inches wide and four inches thick. Post took Gibbon and Andrews by torch light to see the place where it fell. It was about three hundred yards from where Post was standing at the moment of impact.

At the request of Dr. Andrews, the stone was sent to Professor Charles U. Sheppard at the Medical College of South Carolina in Charleston. I could not find any follow-up report from Professor Sheppard.

Lawson Murders

On Brooke Cove Road in Stokes County, North Carolina, on a snowy Christmas Day in 1929, an unspeakable act occurred. The events that took place there just might go down in North Carolina history as the most chilling murders to ever take place in the state. The murders took place at the home of Charlie Lawson on his small tobacco farm in Germanton and left eight people dead and a community shaken.

Just a few days before Christmas, Charles Davis Lawson took his family to nearby Winston-Salem to buy some new clothes and have their picture taken. This seemed a little strange due to the fact that money was in short supply. Little did they know that the clothes they were buying that day would be the clothes that they were buried in.

His daughter, Marie, rose early on Christmas morning to make her signature dessert for Christmas. As she mixed the ingredients for the cake, she had no idea that her time was drawing near. Five years later, the cake was still untouched. It remained on display under glass as a reminder of the massacre.

On Christmas Day, Charlie Lawson, forty-three, murdered his wife and six of their seven children. His first two victims were Carrie, twelve, and Maybell, seven, as they passed the tobacco barn headed to their uncle's house. He returned to the house and shot his wife, Fannie, while she was on the porch. He went inside and shot Marie, seventeen, and then James, four, and Raymond, two. Last was the four-month-old baby, Mary Lou. The oldest son wasn't home; he had been sent to the store to buy some ammunition.

The bodies were laid out with respect. Charlie put each one's pillow under their head and crossed their arms on their chests. He then hid in the nearby woods for more than four hours before doing himself in with a single shot. He had paced around a pine tree so many times that he wore a path in the snow. Officials found some letters near Charlie's dead body that he had written to his parents. What was contained in the letters was never released.

Charlie's brother Elijah and his sons were the first to discover the gruesome scene. They had stopped by on their way home from the morning hunting trip, planning to wish the family a merry Christmas. Word of the tragedy spread quickly. The neighbors began filling up the yard shortly after the police arrived.

There are still unanswered questions about why this horrific event happened. There are several theories. Some say Charlie suffered a head injury when he accidentally hit himself in the head with an axe while remodeling the house. They say he wasn't the same after that. Some say Charlie just went mad. There's a much darker rumor—that Charlie and Marie were engaging in an incestuous relationship, and Marie was pregnant. None of these theories was proven.

The family was laid to rest side by side in a mass grave in Walnut Cove. Because of strict Baptist beliefs, the grave is located outside the hallowed ground of the church. The Lawson family grave and the huge headstone are in the back of the graveyard, completely surrounded by trees.

After the murders, so many people kept coming by the house that one of Lawson's brothers decided to charge twenty-five cents' admission. During the five years that the house was open, sightseers came by the thousands. As for the Christmas cake, one of Lawson's relatives took it home and later buried it.

Many believe that since the family wasn't buried in hallowed ground, their spirits can't find peace. It is reported that nothing, not even the fall leaves, will stay on their grave. People have reported seeing two small children playing in and around the Lawson home. The home was eventually torn down, and the floor boards were used to help build a bridge across a creek that ran through the county. Cars crossing that bridge report strange mists and condensation appearing on the windows, and then small handprints start to appear on the windows.

Arthur, the sole surviving son, married and had four children. He died in a freak truck accident in his early thirties, fifteen years after the murders took place. Stories of premonitions, curses and ghosts increased after Arthur's death.

The portrait of the family that was taken days before Christmas still remains.

A bluegrass song was written about the Lawson family murders and sold to Columbia Records. The song became a hit. A documentary film was released in 2006, titled *A Christmas Family Tragedy*. Booklets, poems and a book, *White Christmas, Bloody Christmas*, written by M. Bruce Jones and Trudy J. Smith, are among the things written about the Lawson family murders.

Lady in Brown

It was a beautiful day in September 1885. From early morning until late evening, you could see the farmers and workers hurrying about the fields in order to get the daily work done.

Every fall, you could see the girls of Northampton County thinking about their upcoming education. They were eagerly preparing for their trip to college. Many families had to endure hardships to get their daughters into college, but they were willing to make whatever sacrifices were needed for their daughters to take advantage of the college opportunities before them.

Chowan University is a small college in Murfreesboro, North Carolina. The school was founded in 1848 as Chowan Baptist Female Institute. It changed names several times before settling on Chowan University in 2006.

Eolene Davidson—a beautiful nineteen-year-old girl, tall with wavy black hair and sparkling blue eyes—was one of the girls planning to attend college. She was the daughter of a well-known and wealthy farmer in Northampton County. Her mother and father were both growing old and tried to give their daughter every advantage they could.

The previous summer, Eolene had spent some time with her friend Margaret Lanston in New York, where she met a young lawyer, James Lorrene. He was twenty-five years old, tall and had black hair. James and Eolene spent much of their time together. As the summer was coming to a close and September was drawing near, Eolene was scheduled to return home to North Carolina. James asked Eolene to marry him. Eolene would have married James, but realizing that her father wanted her to go to college, she turned him down for the time being. Eolene and James agreed that after she had completed her education, they would be married.

Eolene returned home to the quiet fields of Northampton County. The day before she departed for college, she told her mother the story of what happened in New York.

The next morning, as the sun was peeking over the tree tops, Eolene awoke. After the family had their final breakfast, her father hitched the horses and Eolene was on her way. About 11:00 a.m., she reached Murfreesboro. She rode on, finally reaching the stately old building that long stood to welcome the girls. Eolene was given a room on the fourth floor.

She made friends with the other girls but settled down to her work. She soon became a favorite with the teachers and students alike. Eolene was a very popular girl at college. Her favorite dress was made of brown silk that you could hear rustling long before she got to you. Her friends gave her the nickname the "Lady in Brown."

At the end of her first school year, she returned home, looking forward to a joyful summer. Sometime during the summer, James called on Eolene. They were still in love, but Eolene wanted to finish college.

September rolled around, and Eolene returned to school. Sometime in the middle of October, Eolene took sick with a fever. Her many friends waited for her recovery, but Eolene continued to get worse. On Halloween night, Eolene took her last breath. Her body was returned home the next day. Every fall, the freshmen at Chowan are told the story of the Lady in Brown and how you can hear the rustling of her silk dress. For over one hundred years, the Lady in Brown has haunted the dormitory where she lived.

Bolton's Ghost

Fremont, a town on the new railroad line between Wilson and Goldsboro, hosted a festival every summer. Tourists would flock into Fremont from cities near and far to take part in the festival excitement. Many came just for the whiskey that flowed like water all day.

One man, Bolton, was a regular at the festivals. He was a giant of a man and a very heavy drinker. Bolton would perform feats of strength in exchange for whiskey. His main trick was smashing a whiskey barrel to pieces with his head.

At one of the festivals, the crowd was consuming a large amount of whiskey—more than usual. Bolton, like many of the rest, had drunk more than usual. He changed his feats of strength of breaking a few whiskey bottles on his head to breaking two-by-fours on his head, seemingly without pain. The more Bolton drank, the more he bragged until he declared that he could stop a train with his head.

The crowd, almost as drunk as Bolton, cheered him on as he staggered down to the railroad tracks. Bolton stood in the middle of the tracks with his head held down. Before long, the sound of a train whistle in the distance sobered up some of the crowd. Seeing what Bolton was doing, they tried to pull him off the tracks. They were unsuccessful. As the train fast approached Bolton, he just stood there with his head down. He didn't stop the train.

The crowd gathered up the remains of Bolton and took him to the graveyard. They got the local preacher to say a few words over him, and then Bolton was laid to rest.

Shortly after the death of Bolton, a mysterious light was seen rising out of the graveyard and moving to the same spot on the railroad tracks where Bolton breathed his last. Some people say that it's an eerie green glow; others say it's in the shape of a skull. Whatever the shape is, the light will hover around the railroad tracks, and then just before dawn, it will travel back to the same spot in the graveyard that it came from.

Phantom Car

North Carolina 49, which curves through low hills between Asheboro and Charlotte, is no different than many lonely two-lane country roads. It's not a busy road, and you may travel miles before you meet another car. But don't think you're alone—you just might not be.

Sometime in the 1940s (no date given), North Carolina 49 was more isolated and lonely. One night, a family was returning to Charlotte after visiting some relatives. It was late, and all of the family was asleep but the driver. The night was clear and peaceful, and the driver was making good time—as good as you could make in the 1940s. They were alone on the highway. They hadn't passed a car for some time. Out of nowhere, the driver saw lights in the rearview mirror. The car was coming up fast—too fast for the road. The car was on top of the family's car before he noticed it. He hit the brakes and backed off. The driver of the other car kept pulling up close and then backing off while blinking his bright lights.

There was no passing lane and no shoulder for the family to pull off on to let the other car go by. The driver continued to get more and more aggressive. He was now pulling up what seemed to be inches from the family's car and blowing the horn.

Suddenly, and without much thought for his safety, the aggressive driver, ignoring the no passing sign, pulled into the left lane. The place he decided to pass was at the base of one of the Uwharrie Hills. On the other side of the hill, a big panel truck was approaching.

The driver of the car wound it up when the truck came over the hill. With nowhere to go, the family on one side, the truck straight ahead, the car swerved to the left just enough to prevent a head-on collision with the panel truck. The truck hit the side of the car as it was going off the road. The car spun out of control and ended up a twisted, burning mess between two trees. As you might have already guessed, the wild driver of the car expired.

Soon after that fateful night, weary travelers on North Carolina 49 began seeing headlights coming up fast behind them. The car would follow close behind them and then pull into the left lane to pass. At first, the people who see the car notice it's a 1940 Ford with no driver visible. When the car pulls ahead, it just vanishes into the night.

Is the driver of the phantom car still trying to get to his destination? Will he be driving on that road forever?

Ghosts of Gold Hill

The discovery of gold in 1799 on the John Reed farm marked the first gold found in America. The sixteen-pound nugget was used for several years as a door stop. Reed's neighbors, however, convinced him to take it to a Fayetteville jeweler for an appraisal. The jeweler brought Reed some good news: it was gold. A short time later, another nugget was found on the Reed farm weighing twenty-three pounds.

Farmers began searching their farms for gold nuggets. They searched their fields and nearby streams for the valuable ore. In 1823, the government sent Dennis Olmstead, a geologist, to conduct a geological survey in North Carolina.

In 1824, the first gold in the region of Gold Hill was found on the Andrew Troutman farm. As the production of gold in Mecklenburg, Rowan and Cabarrus Counties continued to increase, the government saw a need for a mint in that area. In 1835, President Jackson authorized the Charlotte branch of the United States mint. Approximately 35 percent of total gold coins minted in the United States come from Gold Hill; 89 percent of the gold coins minted come from North Carolina.

In 1842, George Barnhardt leased property at Gold Hill and sank a shaft. In a couple of months, it had reached five hundred feet. In 1855, the Barnhardt shaft changed hands and became known as the Randolph Shaft. The population of Gold Hill reached three thousand. In 1843, the town was incorporated and named Gold Hill. George Barnhardt became Gold Hill's first mayor. The town of Gold Hill was growing. It now had a post office, two general stores, two doctors, a blacksmith, a hotel, a wagon maker, a shoe cobbler, six saloons, two brothels and a much-needed jail.

In 1861, the federal government suspended the use of gold and silver as payment. By the end of 1862, all of the gold and silver coins had disappeared from circulation. In 1907, the mines at Gold Hill closed.

A historical marker in town reads, "Gold discovered here by 1824. Extensive mining begun 1843. Creating a boom town. Copper mined in district until 1907."

In 1989, Historic Gold Hill and Mines Incorporated was formed. The foundation owns seventy acres, including the Barnhardt and Randolph gold mines. It is now known as the Gold Hill Mines Historic Park. Author and historian Vivian Pennington Hopkins is the vice president and director of education for Historic Gold Hill and Mines Foundation.

DEATH AND DISEASE WERE just a part of everyday life in the gold mining industry. Mining was a dangerous job.

One of the spirits haunting Gold Hill is Aaron Klein. Klein was murdered by Stan Cukla in the mine in 1842. He was pushed down an 850-foot shaft. His body was never found. Shortly after his disappearance, a yellow light began being seen near the mouth of the mine. Cukla began acting strange and was seen digging in the bottom of the mine pit; the next day, his body was found. Could Aaron Klein have gotten his revenge?

In January 1954, two witnesses reported a rather frightening sight at the mine. A spirit appeared to them. The only difference from other spirits was that it was in pieces—a head, arms, legs and feet. It was floating and covered in an unearthly light. Then the spirit just vanished. After Walter Newman died in 1918, his ghost was said to haunt the mine and walk the streets of Gold Hill at night.

Aaron Klein and Elizabeth Moyle had fallen in love before his death. Elizabeth never married. Elizabeth's ghost has been reported seen in the mine and near Gold Hill Pond.

An explosion in the powder house impaled one of the miners in the chest with a miner's pick. The miner who died in the powder house is believed to still haunt it.

Two young girls were riding their bikes down to the cemetery when they noticed a beautiful young woman standing on the porch of the old Gold Hill Hotel. It was in bad condition but still standing. As the girls watched

The Gold Hill Ghosts

her, they noticed her dress was blowing in the wind when there was no wind present. Suddenly, they realized they could see right through her. Startled by the woman on the porch, the two girls hurriedly rode away. They never looked back.

Gold Hill has hiking and biking, the Gold Hill rail trail and picnicking. The Montgomery General Store has a bluegrass jam every Friday night.

Banshee of Tar River

Banshees are better known in Scotland and Ireland than in the United States. However, there is one report of a banshee in North Carolina, by the Tar River near Tarboro in Edgecombe County.

The banshee, known as the messenger of death, is also known for its wailing. It is a female spirit in Irish mythology usually seen as an omen of death. The legend goes that a banshee is a woman who begins to wail when someone is about to die.

The Tar River is a great place to catch large catfish or go kayak fishing. It flows into the Pamlico Sound after crossing much of northeast North Carolina. The Tar River travels through fields and small towns and was once a major shipping route for barges loaded with tar. However, the river has a darker side.

Historic Tarboro is located in Edgecombe County and was chartered by the British in 1760. During the Revolutionary War, Dave Warner adopted the Tar River area as his home. He opened and operated a gristmill on the shores of the river. Warner used his grain to help the young Continental army.

One day in August 1781, several people from the nearby town rode to the mill to see Warner. They brought with them a warning: the British were approaching. They warned him to leave, but Warner refused.

The British broke into the mill and found the miller. The redcoats attacked Warner and threatened to drown him. They pinned him to the floor. Faced with the thought of being drowned by the British, Dave Warner warned the

British, "Drown me and you will be haunted by the banshee for the rest of your lives." One British soldier suggested that they wait for the commander to decide the miller's fate, but they decided to go ahead and drown Warner. They chained him and dumped him in the Tar River. As he was sinking into the river, a mist began to roll in and take the form of a woman with long hair. Just then, a blood-curdling scream from what appeared to be a woman echoed from the river.

The soldiers retreated to their camp. By the time the commander made it to the mill, the river had turned black as ink. The officers camped by the mill, and the enlisted men camped by the river. As night slowly crept in, an eerie yellow moon broke through the clouds and cast a yellow glow on the camp. Then the scream of a banshee echoed throughout. Filled with fear, the men confessed to their commander what they had done.

Ashamed of what the soldiers had done, the commander ordered them to work at the mill. One night, the banshee appeared to the men at the mill. She pulled her veil back to expose a horrible face. As the banshee returned to the river, all but one of the soldiers followed her—the one who had instigated the killing of Warner. The men followed the banshee into the river and drowned. The other soldier's body was found days later floating in the river where Warner was drowned.

Since that time, the banshee has made appearances in the month of August, or so the legend says.

Single Brothers House

The Single Brothers House was built in 1769 to house the single brethren of the Moravian congregation of Salem, North Carolina (now Winston-Salem). The first part was designed and built by architect Friedrich Wilhelm Von Marshall. It is now part of the Old Salem National Historic Landmark District, designated in 1966. It was declared an individual National Historic Landmark in 1970. It is part of Old Salem Museum and Gardens and is open as an Old Salem tour building to visitors. It was leased as part of the museum and restored in 1964.

Facing growing pressure from the communities in Pennsylvania, the Moravians relocated to North Carolina. Salem was settled by members of the Moravian Church, a Protestant denomination that first began in 1457 in the kingdoms of Bohemia and Moravia, now part of the Czech Republic. The Moravians bought the site of Salem from Lord Proprietor and Earl of Granville John Carteret in 1753 and founded a religious community. The town was controlled by the church. As the nation grew, the Moravians gradually began to mix into the neighboring communities.

The Single Brothers House was closed in 1823. The oldest part of the building was used as apartments, and the brick addition was used as a boys' school. The school remained open for six years. After the school closed, the building was used for residential purposes and finally became known as the widows' house because mainly single women and widows of the congregation lived there. The Single Sisters took over the property and later leased it in 1964.

On March 26, 1786, Andreas Kresmer was killed while excavating a basement for an addition to the Single Brothers House. There was a cave-in, and Kresmer was buried by the falling dirt. His fellow workers dug him out. Kresmer passed away about 2:00 a.m. after having received the blessing of the congregation. He was a short, kind man and a shoemaker. He was wearing a red cap at the time of his death. Another source says he was wearing a red jacket. On March 27 at 1:00 p.m., Andreas Kresmer was laid to rest in Gods Acre at Old Salem. He was born on March 7, 1753, in Gnadenhutten, Pennsylvania. He moved to North Carolina in October 1766.

Shortly after the death of Kresmer, strange things began to happen at the Single Brothers House. The sound of the tapping of a shoemaker's hammer could be heard. A little man wearing a red cap was seen moving along the hallways. Other times, light footsteps could be heard in the hall. People would sometimes catch a glimpse as Kresmer passed a door.

As the years passed, several citizens were shown the cellar, and to their surprise, the little man in the red cap made an appearance. They tried to catch him but only caught air. The little man in the red cap stood grinning at the door.

So goes the legend that a preacher visited the house and, after hearing the story, invoked the Holy Trinity, "Little man, go to rest!" The spirit has not been seen since.

Ghost of the Taylor House

In Mount Holly, North Carolina, there is an old abandoned house. The Taylor House is located along the bank of the Catawba River in Gaston County.

The house was built in the early to mid-1800s and has been visited once a year by a ghostly figure. The original owners, George and Mathilda Taylor, arrived home after a visit to her mother's. It was late at night on October 25, 1886. George dropped Mathilda off at the house and then headed to the barn to put up the horse and buggy. He heard Mathilda scream. Leaving the horse and buggy, he rushed to Mathilda. When he got into the house, he found her unconscious on the floor.

Standing at the top of the stairs was a blue glow. In the midst of the blue glow was what appeared to be the spirit of a Union soldier. There were holes where the eyes were supposed to be. His left arm was missing and was dripping blue blood. George rushed in. Fear gripped him as the ghost raised its right arm and jumped at him. George picked up his wife and rushed out of the house to the barn. Once Mathilda awoke, they spent the night watching the blue glow move around the house by the windows like it was searching for something.

They decided to stay with Mathilda's mother for a while. George grew tired of the long trip to care for his farm, so he decided to spend a few nights back in his own home without Mathilda. After a few weeks with no ghostly visitor, Mathilda rejoined her husband.

All was well in the house until October 25, 1887. The sound of someone walking in the hallway woke George up at about 11:00 p.m. A blue glow coming under the door caught his attention. Then the ghost started walking down the stairs. The next few hours the ghost spent ransacking the house. All the commotion woke Mathilda. She took one look at George and knew what was downstairs.

George and Mathilda remained in the room for the rest of the night, listening to the ghost going through the house. When daylight came, the ghost vanished. They ventured downstairs and found nothing out of place. George wrote in his journal, "Something evil has driven us from our home." The entry was dated October 26, 1887.

After the Taylors moved out, the house remained empty for almost seven years. Then one day, the Anson family from Tennessee bought the house. They remained in the house for almost twenty years. When Will Anson died of a heart attack, his family packed up and headed back to Tennessee. They didn't bother to return for Will's funeral. The date of Will's death was October 25, 1907. The house was again empty.

The Blake family arrived in mid-September 1926. On the night of October 25, 1927, Sam Blake heard someone moving around in the house. Arming himself with a shotgun, he went out into the hall, coming face to face with the ghost. Before he got a chance to fire, Sam felt something sticky on his foot. He dropped the shotgun and rushed back into the bedroom. Sam and his wife spent the night listening to the ghost searching the house for something.

The following day, Mrs. Blake saw drops of blue blood on the floor and proceeded to clean them up, only to have them reappear. Time and time again she cleaned up the blue blood only to have it reappear. She placed a rug over the blue spots. The next day, the blood had soaked through the rug. After the ghost returned on October 25, 1928, Sam and his wife moved out.

The story goes that each family that lived in the house for the last part of the last century spent October 25 away, giving the spirit the house to continue his search.

The information that I got on this story says that the Taylor House is not the correct name; an alternate name is unknown.

Governor's Mansion Ghost

During much of the colonial period in North Carolina, the governors lived in their own homes. They met in private homes and, when they could get it, the courthouse. In 1722, the assembly selected Edenton, North Carolina, as the capital. This didn't change the living or meeting arrangements. In 1766, New Bern was selected as the government seat. Construction began on the new governor's residence and offices in 1767 and was completed in 1771. Governor Tryon was the first to live in the new governor's house.

During the American Revolution, New Bern was threatened by the enemy. The governor started meeting in different towns, both inland and on the coast. The governor's house, now neglected and falling into disrepair, burned in 1798, all but one wing.

In 1788, a state convention voted to place the capital in Wake County. One thousand acres of Joel Lane's plantation were purchased, and a plan for Raleigh was drawn up. In 1792, construction began on the statehouse. It was first occupied in 1794. The capitol burned in 1831. Construction began on the present capitol building on the same site in 1833 and was completed in 1840 at a total cost of $532,682.34.

In 1888, the supreme court and the state library moved into a separate building. The General Assembly moved into the state legislative building in 1963. The governor and lieutenant governor and their staffs occupy offices on the first floor.

In April 1891, Governor Daniel G. Fowle complained of indigestion so bad that it sent him to bed. His bedroom was on the second floor. Shortly before midnight, Fowle pressed the electric button to summon help. "I feel faint," were the last words the governor said before he dropped his head on his pillow and departed this life. He was ushered to the Oakwood Cemetery, thinking his soul would be at rest. Governor Fowle had ordered an oversized bed but didn't get to enjoy it for long. News of Governor Fowle's death spread quickly across Raleigh.

In 1970, Governor Bob Scott (1969–73) had been living in the governor's mansion for some time. He had grown tired of Fowle's bed. It was time for a new one. His staff moved the old bed out of Scott's room and into a room on the fourth floor and replaced it with a new one.

Shortly after moving the bed, the governor and his wife were in their new bed. Around 10:00 p.m., they heard a strange knocking coming from the wall behind them. It seemed to be coming from where the headboard of Fowle's bed had been. Every night the noise continued until Governor Scott decided to investigate. He learned that Fowle had died in the bed that he had replaced. One theory is that Scott made Fowle mad by moving the bed out of the room. Governor Scott declined to replace the bed according to the ghost's wishes. After Governor Scott moved out, the staff decided to move the old bed back into its original room.

In 1993, Governor Tim Hunt said, "We have a ghost in the mansion. It's the ghost of a previous governor who died in his bed, and I sleep in that bed." Quoted in the *Raleigh News and Observer*, Hunt said that he had not seen the ghost but had heard him.

Pee Dee River Warlock

The Pee Dee River (also known as the Great Pee Dee River) is located in North and South Carolina. It originates in the Appalachian Mountains of North Carolina and is about 435 miles long. It rises as the Yadkin River in the Blue Ridge Mountains of northwestern North Carolina and flows northeast and then southwest to Winyah Bay, Georgetown, South Carolina. The river was named after the Pee Dee Indian tribe.

The people who lived along the Pee Dee River in Richmond County, North Carolina, had evil living among them. His name was Harvey, and he was a warlock (a man who professes or is supposed to practice magic or sorcery). By the time they found out, he was already an old man.

Over a period of time, he got to know the farmers and their families in the small area. He would ask for milk and flour and other small items. The farmers were kind enough to give it to him. But his requests became greater and greater and then became demands. If his demands were not met, the farmers suffered horrible consequences.

One day while neighbor Sally was milking her cow, Harvey dropped in uninvited. Harvey demanded that Sally give him the cow. Sally refused Harvey's demands. Harvey told Sally that from this date on the cow would never do her any good.

The following day, Sally found that her cow had stopped eating and was giving blood instead of milk. The cow continued to lose weight and give blood instead of milk until Sally finally gave up and gave the cow to Harvey. The next day, Sally went to check on the cow and found that it

Pee Dee River Warlock

was eating and giving milk. Angrily, Sally threatened to take her cow back. Harvey told her that if she took the cow back, it would die before she got her home. Sally left, but not before she told Harvey not to come back to her farm.

After a few weeks, Harvey returned to Sally's farm while she was feeding her hog. Angrily, she ordered Harvey to get off her farm. Harvey agreed—if she would give him the hog. She refused, and he left, but not before he told her the hog would do her no good. The hog suddenly dropped dead.

Sally asked her neighbor's advice. He suggested that she draw a picture of Harvey and shoot it where she wanted him to feel pain. She drew a picture of Harvey and attached it to the barn. She shot the picture in the shoulder. When she visited Harvey again, she found that he had a problem with his shoulder. Sally felt that he deserved what he got. She shot the drawing again and again.

She visited Harvey again and found him seriously ill. Feeling she had punished him enough, she decided to take down the drawing. On her way home, a storm came up. Sally went into the house for safety, forgetting about the drawing. Lightning struck the barn and burned it down, along with the drawing.

The next day, Sally hurried to Harvey's place to see what his condition was. When she arrived, she discovered a crowd had gathered around his house. She got to Harvey in time to hear his last wish: he wanted to be buried under the walnut tree between his dog and mule and to be buried after dinner. His last words were, "When lightning strikes the walnut tree, then you'll know I'm in hell."

As requested, the neighbors buried Harvey under the walnut tree. Due to an eerie storm approaching, the neighbors scattered and returned home. That very evening, a bolt of lightning hit the walnut tree. Did Harvey finally meet the devil like he said he would?

Blood Showers

On February 15, 1850, a shower of fresh blood rained down near the home of Thomas M. Clarkson in Sampson County, North Carolina. It was about 50 feet wide and 250 to 300 yards long. Clarkson lived on a farm about thirteen miles southwest of Clinton. This was stated in a letter to the *North Carolinian* newspaper in Fayetteville.

The wife of Kit Lasater, who lived on the farm of Silas Beckwith in the New Hope Township in Chatham County, North Carolina, stated that at about two o'clock on Monday, February 25, 1884, while near her cabin, a shower of blood fell around her from a cloudless sky. Mrs. Lasater heard what she thought was a heavy rain. She looked up and could only see a clear blue sky. When she looked down, she saw what appeared to be the aftermath of a shower of blood. None of the blood fell on Mrs. Lasater, but it drenched the ground and surrounding trees for about sixty feet. After hearing the story about the blood rain, the neighbors rushed to Mrs. Lasater's home to see for themselves.

Dr. Sidney Atwater gathered up some of the liquid-stained sand and leaves and took them to the University of North Carolina at Chapel Hill. There, he turned it over to Professor Francis Preston Venable to be analyzed. In almost every test, the conclusion was the same: it appeared to be blood. Professor Venable was one of the most accomplished scientists of his day. In 1884, he wrote a serious scientific paper claiming that a large amount of blood seemed to have fallen out of the sky onto a small piece of land in Chatham County. What kind of blood remains unknown. More than a century has passed since Professor Venable analyzed the blood. Scientists are still at a loss to explain how blood rained down from the sky.

For millennia, showers of blood have been reported in sources both historical and literary. The earliest recorded account is from Homer's *Iliad* when Zeus made it rain blood.

Henkelite Cemetery

Henkelite Cemetery, also known as the Lutheran Union Church Cemetery, is the final resting place for many Confederate soldiers. The cemetery is located in Mount Pleasant, Cabarrus County, North Carolina. It has forty-six interments dating back to 1825. Confederate flags are still flying to honor those who fought in the Civil War.

Most of the headstones are cracked or broken with age, and many have eroded until they are unreadable. The steeple placed in the cemetery is from the old Holy Trinity Lutheran Church from 1878. It is now deteriorating.

Like most cemeteries, this one has a ghost story. There have been reports of ghostly sounds of gunfire and Confederate soldiers marching. Some have witnessed the ghosts of Confederate soldiers standing guard in their military uniforms, guarding the cemetery. Some say pictures have been taken showing children playing when no children were there. At least six children are buried there. On occasion, vehicles will not start when attempting to leave the cemetery.

Cary's Phantom Horse

Cary, North Carolina, has a scenic downtown district that is perfect for a cozy little stroll on a fall afternoon. Don't be surprised if you hear the ghostly hoofbeats of a phantom horse running down Academy Street. The legend of the phantom horse dates back to 1865. The website www. candidslice.com said the story came from Kris Carmichael, director of the Page Walker Arts and History Center.

With all the southerners still in an uproar over the Civil War, it just made matters worse when Colonel Oscar Jackson and his Union soldiers took over the Page homestead shortly after fighting ended. The citizens of Cary were outraged. The soldiers used the main house as a hospital.

The morning of the Union army's departure, as the troops were preparing to leave the Page homestead, a soldier was given the job of taking the horse of a Union soldier that had died with him. The horse managed to escape and run off. No one could find the missing horse, so the soldiers left without it.

Years passed, and the horse was forgotten. In the late 1860s, Tom Sanderson was the stable boy at the Page Walker Hotel. One evening, he was alone in the stable when suddenly, the horses began to panic. Sanderson heard the sound of a horse running at full speed outside. Sanderson went outside to meet the rider, but the road was empty. Sanderson has told the story of the phantom horse to generations of hotel visitors. Several people have reported hearing the phantom horse running through downtown Cary.

Is this the phantom horse that once belonged to the Union soldier who died?

Ghost of Joe McGee

North Carolina was home to America's first gold rush. The state would remain America's leading producer of gold until the discovery in California in 1848. For nearly forty years, North Carolina supplied the United States mint with a substantial part of its gold.

Gold was discovered on the Reed farm in 1799 when Reed's son Conrad discovered a large yellow rock in the creek that ran across the farm. The Reeds didn't realize what they had and used the unusual rock as a doorstop until 1802. A jeweler from Fayetteville was passing through, saw the rock and recognized it as gold. He paid Reed $3.50 for it. John Reed would later discover the rock was worth $3,500 when the jeweler returned to buy more rocks. Reed would get another $1,000 for the first rock.

Word of the discovery of gold on the Reed farm quickly spread, and the corner of Cabarrus County was invaded by prospectors from around the world. Reed's farm would become the center of gold fever. Mining experts from Cornwall, England, were brought in to set up and oversee daily operations. Labor had to be imported from around the world to keep up with the work.

Land near the Reed farm where gold was also discovered was owned by a man named McIntosh. McIntosh was a thrifty, grumpy old man. With all his gold, he refused to pay his workers enough money or provide them with the tools needed to keep them safe. He became known as a miserly old codger called Skinflint.

McIntosh sought the services of an expert miner named Joe McGee. McGee knew McIntosh's reputation and did not feel he would get paid what he was worth. So for McGee to go to work for McIntosh, they made a deal. If Joe McGee died while working in the mine, McIntosh would pay McGee's wife, Jennie, $2,000.

One night, McGee didn't come home at his regular time. Sometime later, McGee still hadn't come home. His wife became worried and got all of his friends, and they searched the mine looking for McGee. The search was completed with no sign of McGee. After several weeks, Jennie McGee asked McIntosh for the $2,000 she was promised. McIntosh refused to give it to her because McGee's body could not be found. McIntosh said that McGee had run away.

Soon after McIntosh refused to pay Jennie, McGee's friend Shaun heard a knocking on his cabin door late one night. When Shaun opened the cabin door, there stood a ghostly figure that spoke to him in the voice of Joe McGee. The ghostly figure told Shaun to dig in the place in the mine where the green timbers gave way and caused a cave-in, and his body would be found. The ghostly figure asked if McIntosh had paid his wife the $2,000 that she was owed. Shaun answered, "No." The ghostly figure wailed, "I'll haunt that mine forever." Then the figure disappeared into the darkness.

That night, Shaun went back to the mine and dug where the ghostly figure had told him to dig. He found Joe McGee's body. With the finding of McGee's body, McIntosh had to pay Jennie her money. McGee kept his promise and haunted the mine forever, scaring away all the workers. McIntosh could not find anyone to work in his mine because of the terrifying white figure that appeared wailing deep in the mine. He died a poor man.

Crybaby Lane

On May 3, 1900, Sister Mary Agnes Price became the postmaster of the new post office in the Raleigh area. It was named Nazareth for the Catholic orphanage located in Raleigh near Bilyeu Street and Western Boulevard. Father Thomas Frederick Price founded the Catholic orphanage in 1898. He was the first North Carolina native to be ordained a Catholic priest. He was ordained in 1886 and wanted to start an orphanage and seminary. Four miles outside of what was then the Raleigh city limits, Father Price was granted permission by Bishop Haid, the vicar of the Apostolic Church of North Carolina, to start an orphanage. The Nazareth Orphanage started sheltering Catholic and Protestant boys in 1898. The seminary followed in 1902. With the need for a place for girls, Nazareth Orphanage eventually started accepting girls.

It seems that nobody can agree on the date of the fires—1903, 1905, 1912, 1958 or 1961. The fire starting in 1905 led to a gruesome ghost story that is still told today. The legend states that the orphanage burned to the ground, taking the lives of many children with it.

Another legend of the 1905 fire says it started at 2:00 a.m. on October 29, 1905, and consumed the priests' living quarters. Priest John Gladdish and one young man were killed when they jumped from a third-story window.

In the 1912 fire at Nazareth, a dormitory, a schoolroom, the stables and a barn were destroyed, and a wildfire started in the nearby woods. No one died in the 1912 fire.

The most tragic tale of the orphanage fires comes from 1958. A fire broke out in one of the orphanage dormitories. By the time the sleeping children became aware of the fire, it was too late. When the fire department arrived, the building was reduced to burnt beams. Many of the children burned to death inside the building. I could not find any reliable record of this fire.

The 1961 fire was started accidentally by a priest. Priest Raymond J. Donohue was attempting to get rid of some wasp nests from the eaves of one of the buildings by setting them on fire, and he burned the building to the ground. The building was used as the rectory, and there were no children in the building at the time of the fire.

At its biggest point, Nazareth Orphanage occupied several hundred acres. The church in later years began to sell or donate some of its property. The remaining buildings of the Nazareth Orphanage remained in use until 1975, when Bishop F. Joseph Grossman converted the facility into the Catholic Center of the Diocese.

Some of the strange stories attached to the orphanage include reports that months after the fire occurred and the remains of the damaged buildings were torn down and hauled away, people began complaining to city officials about the strong smell of smoke. People still complained about choking on smoke even though new grass covered the area. There were also the voices coming out of the air of children crying and wailing in pain. The sounds of those who died in the fire can still be heard.

There's one about the gatekeeper who guards the entrance to Crybaby Lane and the shadowy figure in the woods. While there was an orphanage near what's called Crybaby Lane, there was never an orphanage, and no children died on Crybaby Lane. Crybaby Lane is off Bilyeu and is just a piece of undeveloped land.

Sometimes when retelling a story, truth and fiction get mixed together. Crybaby Lane is a good example of how local memories can get distorted in a good ghost story and become just another folk tale. The facts are distorted and shrouded in mystery. This story still circulates around Halloween.

Payne Road

If you grew up near the Rural Hill area of Forsyth County, North Carolina, you've probably heard of the legend of Payne Road. The road is long, dark and in the middle of the country. There are decaying buildings, winding curves and a presence in the air. A correction in the legend's location asserts that the road where the legends are based is actually called Edwards Road, not Payne Road. However, there is a road in the same area called Payne Road.

There are three different stories tied to the haunting. It seems that no one can agree on what really happened or where it happened, Edwards Road or Payne Road. For now, I am going to use Payne Road as the setting. The first story is the most famous. Edward Payne owned a large plantation in the area. One day, he found out that his daughter was expecting, and the father was one of his slaves. Payne murdered the slave and descended into what some called devil worship. Payne later found out that another one of his daughters had been with a slave. Some say Payne lost it and murdered the slave, then murdered the slave's entire family. Then Payne set fire to the plantation, killing the remaining slaves. Another version is that Payne turned to Satanism and sacrificed the slaves as evil tokens. Stories of devil worship are tied to the legends.

The second legend has ties to Payne Road, not the land around it. The story goes that a young man was driving down Payne Road and didn't make the curve. He wrecked near where the chapel once stood where Edward Payne worshiped the devil. The young man died a slow, painful death as onlookers stood by and did nothing to help the victim trapped in the burning car. Some say if you drive down Payne Road late at night, you can see the round headlights of a Ford following you around the curve where the young man met his fiery death. A little way down the road, the lights will vanish.

Milus Frank Edwards (1882–1955) was the landowner of the area that is synonymous with the legends. This area is two miles up Edwards Road on one of the sharp curves. Edwards made threats on his own life over financial problems. On October 5, 1955, Edwards parked his pickup in a shed that was across the road from his house. He took out a stick of dynamite, held it up to his head, lit it and blew himself up. It was reported that Edwards had four other siblings who had done themselves in. He was buried in Crestview Memorial Park Rural Hill in Forsyth County.

Peggy, who grew up in the area in the 1930s and 1940s, remembered Payne Road as just another road. In 1991, vandals burned the Edwards house to the ground. As the years have gone by, nature has reclaimed what was left of the Edwards house after the fire. All that's left is the chimney. In the 2000s, Edwards Road was completely paved. Several decaying houses and a church along Payne Road have been vandalized and burned by teenagers and devil worshipers.

Haunted Bentonville Battlefield

The largest Civil War battle in North Carolina was the Battle of Bentonville, which took place on March 19–21, 1865, in Johnston County. It was one of the last attempts to defeat the Union cavalry before the South fell. Confederate general Joseph E. Johnston made one last desperate attempt to stop Union general William T. Sherman's drive through the Carolinas in the last days of the Civil War.

Reports came that General Sherman's sixty thousand Union soldiers were marching toward Goldsboro, North Carolina, destroying everything in their path. This news caused General Johnston to concentrate his band of Confederate soldiers, about twenty-one thousand, near Bentonville. Johnston's Confederate soldiers attacked one of General Sherman's three wings at Bentonville on March 18, driving them back before a counterattack by General Sherman's cavalry halted the advance. More Union cavalry arrived, giving General Sherman nearly three to one over General Johnston's troops.

On March 19, General Johnston deployed his troops across and above Goldsboro Road. On the left was General Braxton Bragg's command, Hokes division, which included the seventeen- and eighteen-year-olds from the North Carolina Junior Reserves. On the right were Lieutenant General William J. Hardee's veterans of the Tennessee Army. On the morning of March 19, the Confederate cavalry was again attacked by the Union cavalry. After several strikes failed to budge the Union cavalry, the Confederate army withdrew to its original lines at sundown.

By 4:00 p.m. on March 20, most of the Union right wing had reached Bentonville. General Johnston was forced to deploy the cavalry to give a strong appearance. After several skirmishes on March 21, the Confederate army escaped from Bentonville that night and returned to Smithfield. General Wade Hampton's cavalry covered its retreat. Total casualties at Bentonville were 1,527 Union and 2,606 Confederates. A month later, General Johnston surrendered his cavalry to General Sherman.

The Harper House was commandeered as a hospital.

THE GHOSTS OF THE BATTLE OF BENTONVILLE

There have been reports of a ghostly reenactment of a battle near the Harper House. One night in late March 1905, two men, Jim Weaver and Joe Lewis, were out possum hunting, as they occasionally did. Thinking their dog had treed a possum, Weaver decided to cut down a small tree that was in the way. To their surprise, when the axe hit the tree, they saw a bright flash of light coming from the top of the tree. That was followed by more flashes in the woods. They saw shadowy figures of soldiers and heard the sound of horses' hooves as they went by them. They saw a Union soldier trying to take a Confederate flag from a soldier. The Confederate soldier had a wound in his shoulder and fell to the ground. As the two hunters made a hasty retreat from the woods, they went past the Harper House, where they said they saw strange lights in the windows.

This story has an unusual ending. When Weaver was telling the story of what they saw in the woods that night, there was one person who knew Weaver was telling the truth: a Civil War veteran whose useless left arm was a reminder of that night in 1865 when a seventeen-year-old boy suffered a wound in the shoulder fighting to keep the flag.

There have been reports of strange disembodied sounds of shouting and ghostly gunfire heard, and a ghostly Confederate/Union battle has been seen taking place in the woods.

Near the Harper House is a cemetery where visitors have reported capturing strange lights in pictures and recording EVPs (electronic voice phenomenon).

Fiery ghosts have been seen in the windows of the Harper House. People have had the feeling that something was trying to push them down the stairs. From time to time, the lights in the house go on and off by themselves when everything is locked up. The face of Mr. Harper has been seen looking out from a window. A ghostly fire inside the house with shadowy figures walking around it has been reported.

Bentonville Battleground Park was founded in 1965 and was declared a national historic landmark in 1996.

Haunted Mordecai House

The Mordecai House was built in 1785 on a large plantation in North Carolina. The plantation was once the largest in Wake County, covering approximately five thousand acres. The plantation house was built by Joel Lane for his son Henry Lane. Joel Lane was one of the instrumental figures in the establishment of Raleigh as the first planned state capital in the United States. The Mordecai House is the oldest house in Raleigh still in its original location. The Mordecai House got its name when Moses Mordecai married into the Lane family in 1817. He first married Margaret Lane, who later died in 1824. He then married her younger sister, Ann Lane.

The descendants of Moses Mordecai lived in the house for five more generations. The house was willed to the City of Raleigh in 1964. Now the Mordecai House is part of and located in Raleigh's Mordecai Square Historic Park.

During the Civil War, the plantation where the Mordecai House is located was the site of many battles. Many soldiers on both sides died in the battles on the property. Some believe that the wandering souls of both Confederate and Union soldiers who died there still haunt the land and the Mordecai House.

Visitors and employees report seeing a woman in the hallway wearing a long black skirt, a white blouse and a black tie. She can also be seen standing on the balcony if you go by the Mordecai House late at night. Some believe the ghostly apparition of one of the Lane girls can be seen and heard playing the piano. Others believe the ghostly figure is Mary Willis Mordecai Turk, who lived in the house from 1858 to 1937. She appears as a ghostly figure in a gray nineteenth-century dress. Some visitors have reported occasionally seeing a gray mist hovering near the piano.

People have reported seeing strange things while on tours. When the tour guide points at a historic portrait of the home's previous owner and speaks the person's name, the portrait suddenly falls off the wall or flies across the room.

Ghostly footsteps can often be heard when no one is there. They are heard in the upstairs rooms or on the stairs. Staff members have reported hearing the footsteps after the place is closed. One employee reported seeing things move.

The Mordecai House was featured on an episode of the Syfy channel's *Ghost Hunters*.

Other historic buildings in the park include the overseer's office, the smokehouse, the Allen kitchen, the Badger- Iredell Law Office, the St. Mark Chapel and the birthplace of the seventeenth president, Andrew Johnson. The visitors' center is located on the first floor of the Mordecai House.

Legend of Peter Dromgoole

G imghoul Castle is located about a half mile east of Davis Library at the end of Gimghoul Road. It was originally known as Hippol Castle. It was built in the 1920s for about $50,000 and took between four and six years to complete. Artisans from France were hired to cut the thirteen tons of stone used to build the castle in Chapel Hill, North Carolina. The 2.15 acres of land are owned by the Order of Gimghoul, a nonprofit organization for men. The castle was built on the site of the alleged death of Peter Dromgoole.

For nearly two centuries, the legend of Peter Dromgoole has enchanted the students at the University of North Carolina at Chapel Hill. There are several legends that go along with Gimghoul Castle and Peter Dromgoole. In the more romantic version, Peter Dromgoole got into an argument with another student in 1833 over a girl known simply as Miss Fanny. The two gentlemen decided to settle it in a gentlemanly way: with a duel. They met at the appointed time and place, took their positions and fired. Peter Dromgoole fell on a boulder from the bullet. He lay there dying in Miss Fanny's arms, his blood spilled on the rock that would conceal his lifeless body for all eternity. The duel was held at Piney Prospect on the University of North Carolina at Chapel Hill campus. A shallow grave was dug, and Peter Dromgoole's body was placed in it. The rock that Dromgoole's blood spilled on was placed on top of the grave. The bloodstains are said to still be visible on the rock to this day.

Another version of this story is that Miss Fanny was not at the duel. She began to wonder where Dromgoole had disappeared to. Miss Fanny was heartbroken and returned to their favorite spot to wait for him. Dromgoole never met Miss Fanny there again. She sat on the rock that Dromgoole was buried under every day and cried. The story goes on to say that Miss Fanny later died heartbroken. The shadowy figures of Miss Fanny's and Peter Dromgoole's ghosts still meet there. They are Chapel Hill's most famous spirits.

Students who told many versions of the legend of the duel formed a secret society in 1889 called the Order of Gimghoul. In 1926, construction was completed on the Gothic edifice called Hippol Castle at Piney Prospect.

Peter Dromgoole was born in Halifax County of Irish ancestry. He was the son of a Virginia planter who had strong ties to North Carolina. Dromgoole was never a student at the University of North Carolina at Chapel Hill. He arrived there in January 1833 and failed the entrance exam but was allowed to stay around working with a tutor. He fell in with less than desirable company. Legend says that Dromgoole left for Europe never to be seen or heard from again. There is supposedly a letter written from Dromgoole to his father saying that he would go to Europe and never come back.

One source says that in the summer of 1833, Peter Dromgoole joined the army at Southport. He then called Smithville home using the assumed name of Williams.

In E.T. Malone's book *Dromgoole, Twice Murdered*, he describes the details of Dromgoole's life. Under the name John Williams, he joined the army in Wilmington, North Carolina, and was sent to Florida to serve in the Seminole Indian uprising. He quickly rose to the rank of sergeant. His unfortunate demise was at the hands of a Private Samuel Wright, who was drunk at the time he killed Williams. Peter Dromgoole, also known as John Williams, is buried in St. Augustine, Florida.

The real story of Peter Dromgoole has been twisted over the decades.

Charlotte Fire Station No. 4

The City of Charlotte bought the property for Charlotte Fire Station No. 4 in 1925 for $1,000 from Cornelia Tae and T.B. Whitted. The station was designed by Charles Christian Hook, an architect of local and regional importance. The design is reflective of the architectural design of firehouses in the 1920s. Fire Station No. 4 was built in 1925–26 and opened on April 1, 1926. West Fifth Street was chosen for Fire Station No. 4 to better serve downtown's fire protection with proximity to the center of the city and the Fourth Ward neighborhood. Charlotte Fire Station No. 4 served as a fire station until 1972, when it was replaced by a new fire station that is still in use.

The old Fire Station No. 4 has been used for several different things over the years, such as for storage by the city sanitation department, an art gallery, offices and the Charlotte-Mecklenburg Fire Museum.

The building was also featured in an FBI sting operation that netted a former mayor of Charlotte. An undercover agent solicited the mayor's help navigating bureaucracy to get a business started there.

On April 1, 1934, firefighter Pruitt L. Black was getting dressed on the second floor to respond to a fire. He was headed to the pole to slide down to the first floor when he tripped on his firefighter britches and fell through the hole to the first floor, fracturing his skull. Black died a short time later at age twenty-eight.

Visitors to the fire station often commented on Black's ghostly appearance, which was usually accompanied by the distinctive smell of his cigar smoke.

Other visitors have reported smelling cigar smoke on the second level when no one was around.

Charlotte Fire Station No. 4 was added to the National Register of Historic Places on December 20, 2016.

Seven Hearths Ghosts

Seven Hearths is a beautiful home situated on King Street. It is located in Hillsborough's historic district in Orange County, North Carolina. The house dates to sometime in the first half of the eighteenth century; the exact date is unknown.

The house was originally built as a tavern, William Reed's Ordinary, which was in operation from colonial times to the early days of the republic. Sometime before the beginning of the nineteenth century, the tavern became the private residence of the Hayes family. William Reed's Ordinary had sold its last spirit. The house began being called Seven Hearths. The Hayes family lived there from the early nineteenth century into the middle of the twentieth century.

They had a daughter named Jane Hayes. Jane was only sixteen years old when she died of an unknown illness. One source says she died of consumption in 1854.

Since her death, residents have reported seeing the semitransparent figure of a young girl with long hair wearing a wispy nightgown. She has been seen wandering from room to room. People walking by the house have reported that at times they can see a semitransparent young girl looking out of the upstairs window.

Another ghost that haunts Seven Hearths is a bit on the unusual side. It is believed to be the ghost of Dr. William Hayes, who had his doctor's office in the house during the 1920s. Dr. Hayes was a Spiritualist. He believed that humans were reincarnated as animals after their deaths.

Apparently, he was well on his way to proving he was right after he died. There have been rumors of a tabby cat with the head of a human roaming the halls of Seven Hearths.

When the Hayes family sold Seven Hearths, they told the new owners about the ghostly residents. The new owners have encountered both ghosts.

Seven Hearths later changed owners again. The new owners have restored the outside of the house closer to what it looked like when it was William Reed's Ordinary. They have not said if they have met the ghostly residents.

Have the ghosts of Jane Hayes and Dr. William Hayes finally found peace?

The central block of the house is an excellent example of early Piedmont architecture. The west wing of the house was probably built in the 1820s.

All of the early owners of the house, William Reed, Barnaby Cabe, William Courtney and Thomas Watts, have been significant figures in local history.

Carolina Inn

The distinguished Carolina Inn was built in 1924 next to the University of North Carolina–Chapel Hill to house visitors to the university. The architecture of the building was patterned after George Washington's home in Mount Vernon. The Carolina Inn was built by university trustee John Sprunt Hill. The inn was designed by award-winning architect Arthur C. Nash. The Carolina Inn is an extravagantly detailed historic inn that is just oozing with southern charm. Since its opening in 1924, it has served as a hospitable and cheerful inn.

When the inn was completed in December 1924, it was a modern structure. It had an all-electric kitchen, a commercial ice maker and an elevator.

In 1935, John Sprunt Hill donated the inn to the university with the provision that the inn's profits be donated to the university to help with the upkeep of the university's library.

The inn has been through five major renovations since it was built. The Carolina Inn is listed in the National Register of Historic Places and is a member of the National Trust's Historic Hotels of America. It serves its guests with its share of tradition and four-star diamond services. It resembles a country estate more than an inn. It has 184 guest rooms and suites, 2 VIP king suites, 4 deluxe queen suites and 1 deluxe double queen suite.

The Carolina Crossroads Restaurant offers progressive new American cuisine. It is renowned for its gourmet fare, contemporary menus and southern flair. The Carolina Inn also offers meeting and banquet space and a ballroom that seats three hundred people. It has many other amenities. The Carolina Inn has been an iconic destination since its opening in Chapel Hill.

In holding with tradition, there has to be a ghost or two in a hotel this old.

Dr. William Jacocks was a physician with the International Health Division of the Rockefeller Foundation. From 1948 to 1965, when he died, room 252 was his room. Since renovations, room 252 is now 256. Suite 252, where Dr. William Jacocks lived for seventeen years, is believed to be haunted by the good doctor. He is said to be a friendly ghost and very welcoming. Guests have experienced the overwhelming smell of fresh flowers even though there were no flowers in the room. Other guests have reported the strong smell of cologne. Dr. Jacocks likes to lock guests out of room 252. There was one occasion when the door to room 252 had to be taken down because it would not open. Electronic locks were installed in 1990, but there are still complaints of the door refusing to unlock. There are reports of curtains being pulled open when no one is there. There are also reports of cold spots in the room. The shower mat becomes crumpled like someone is standing on it. There was one time when both handles of the faucet fell off. One guest reported hearing a loud whizzing sound when the air conditioner was not on. Guests have reported mysterious knocking on the walls. Another reported something shook the bed. There have been reports of doors closing on their own.

Some staff members have reported seeing a man appear in a black suit with a blue overcoat and a knit hat. Some report that he goes from door to door wiggling the doorknobs like he's trying to find an open door. Some guests have reported hearing the doorknob wiggle and open the door just to see him disappear right in from of them.

Some guests have reported hearing a piano playing when there was no music playing and no piano around. Others have heard footsteps and disembodied voices, and orbs have been photographed. People have reported bumping into a person only to find out there's no one there.

All of the ghosts at the Carolina Inn appear to be friendly. Some say the inn is home to as many as twenty ghosts.

First Presbyterian Church

After Charlotte's incorporation in 1768, the city was without a church for almost fifty years. Church services were held with alternating ministers in the county courthouse. In 1815, the commissioners set aside a plot of land to be used to build a church. Construction on the brick church started in 1818 and was completed in 1823. The church was dedicated soon after. It was called the Brick Church or the Town Church. Most just called it the Presbyterian Church. Charlotte had a predominant Ulster-Scot Presbyterian base. By 1826, a bell had been added to the church. The original bell survived and is now on display in a frame in the foyer between the sanctuary and the chapel. The original church Bible from 1853 survived the ravages of time and is on display in a glass case in the foyer along with the bell.

The Presbyterian Church of Charlotte was officially recognized as a congregation on September 5, 1821. In 1841, the Presbyterian congregation acquired the town church property and renamed it the First Presbyterian Church.

By the 1850s, the congregation had outgrown the original church, and in 1857, it built another church. This one was a Gothic Revival church built with bricks and covered with stucco and painted in imitation of cut stone. The church was 50 feet wide, 80 feet long and had balconies on both sides. The steeple was 187 feet high.

By the 1890s, the First Presbyterian Church congregation had outgrown the building again. The congregation decided to extend the church about twenty feet. During 1894 and 1895, the side walls and rear wall were found to be structurally unsound. They were removed and rebuilt, keeping only the rear balcony in the sanctuary. The church was also fitted with three large gas/electric chandeliers. The First Presbyterian Church was included in the National Register of Historic Places in 1982.

THE GHOST OF AMBROSE

Ambrose was the name of one of the church's janitors during the Civil War. When General Sherman and his Union army were nearing Charlotte in 1863, the elders asked Ambrose to dig a tunnel under what is now Fifth Street to hide the silver offering trays and other church valuables. After the Union army left, the elders asked Ambrose to go down in the tunnel and get the pieces that he had placed down there. When Ambrose entered the tunnel, it caved in. Ambrose was buried.

Members of the church congregation and employees of the church have reported seeing Ambrose. Some have reported feeling him in the church sanctuary. One of the church employees saw Ambrose and thought he was a current sexton, but when he called to him, Ambrose disappeared.

They say there are other signs that Ambrose is around, such as the chandeliers in the sanctuary tinkling and light bulbs exploding. Others say that Ambrose has been seen in the stairwell.

A person passing the First Presbyterian Church saw a white figure passing to and fro in front of the church. The figure did this time and time again. It created great interest and speculation. The March 10, 1876 edition of the *Daily Charlotte Observer* ran a headline, "A Ghost in a Church Yard." The story had a simple ending. The "ghost" was a man under a sheet with a pole, and he raised or lowered the sheet to the desired height. Not everything we see is what it appears to be.

Queens University

The Charlotte Female Institute (1857–91) was founded in downtown Charlotte. It is now located in Myers Park, three miles from its original location. In 1891, it became the seminary for girls (1891–96). Its name changed to the Presbyterian Female College (1896–1912). In 1912, it became the Queens College and moved to Myers Park. In 1930, Queens College linked to the Presbyterian Synod of South Carolina through a merger with Chicora College.

In the 1940s, the school began to admit men. Shortly after World War II, men could attend the college but not stay on campus. In 1948, Queens College opened a co-ed evening college. In 1987, it become fully co-ed, allowing men to live on campus. In 2002, Queens College became Queens University of Charlotte.

Now for the ghost stories. Every college seems to have its resident ghosts. Apparently, students, staff and faculty at Queens University have reported sighting of ghosts over the years. They have reported everything from phantom screams to visions of Civil War soldiers. Most of the ghosts at Queens University are speculated to be those of students who "did themselves in" while attending the university.

Under the Dana Auditorium on the main campus is the Suzanne Little Rehearsal Hall, where students practice before performances. Many students have reported a well-dressed lady who walks past them and then vanishes.

In the Hall Brown, also known as the Overcash Hall, students claim room 303 is haunted. One night, a student woke up to find her roommate slumped over her desk. She tried to wake her roommate but couldn't do so. She noticed her hair and realized it was not her roommate. She screamed, and the figure disappeared. Her real roommate woke up, startled from her sleep. She had been in bed sleeping all along.

The Albright Residence Hall is haunted by a girl who committed suicide in the dorm. The story goes that the girl cut her wrist out of shame. As she lay dying on the bed, she wrote "Julie," the name of her friend, on the wall. Some students claim the dead girl's spirit wanders the halls with blood dripping from her wrists. Students have said that "Julie" written in blood mysteriously appears on the wall in her room. The door to the room reportedly flies open on its own. A knocking sound on the walls has been heard by students.

Wallace Residence Hall students have reported cold spots in the corner of a dorm room, along with strange clanging and knocking noises.

The Main Courtyard is haunted by the spirits of several Civil War soldiers. Students have also heard screaming coming from somewhere on the grounds. The apparition of a person hanging from a tree has been reported. A male student supposedly hanged himself from a tree.

Female students claim to see the ghost of a little girl throughout the Belk Residence Hall. Another student was awakened in the middle of the night by a violent shaking in her room. She woke up to find the desk next to her bed moving. The desk stopped as mysteriously as it had started. She looked around the desk and could find nothing that would make it shake. She went back to bed, only to have the desk start shaking again. She tried to get out of the room but watched as the door locked itself. Next, the face of a little girl appeared on the closet door.

Burwell Hall is another haunted place. Adelaide, who graduated from Queens in 1961 and has worked at the university for over thirty years, tells of an incident in 1913 when a female employee was working late. She saw a woman walk past the door of her office and went to find out who the woman was. The woman turned and said, "You should not be working in this building after 10:00 p.m." Later, when Adelaide saw the portrait of Mrs. Burwell hanging in the building, she realized that was who she saw, but Mrs. Burwell had been dead for years.

Stonewall Jackson Reform School

The Stonewall Jackson Youth Development Center was a juvenile correctional facility that opened in 1909 in Concord. It was the first juvenile correctional facility in North Carolina. The school was established as a place to house young juveniles who had committed crimes.

In the late nineteenth century, young boys who were convicted of minor crimes were treated with the same punishment as hardened adult criminals. In 1890, James P. Cook, editor of the local daily newspaper, the *Standard*, witnessed a thirteen-year-old boy convicted of petty theft being sentenced to three years and six months at hard labor on the Cabarrus County chain gang. The boy was taken from the courtroom chained to a convicted adult criminal. The boy had taken $1.30 from distant relatives who had agreed to care for the boy after his parents died.

For the next seventeen years, Cook campaigned for the establishment of a training school for underage boys. Cook's work steadily changed the hearts and minds of the citizens of North Carolina. The organization King's Daughters of North Carolina was on board with the idea. Supporters convinced the North Carolina legislature to embrace their idea. A special committee of the King's Daughters in 1906 successfully campaigned for the school. They held public meetings, wrote newspaper articles and editorials and handed out pamphlets describing how successfully that program was working in other states.

Sponsors of the bill gained the support of the Confederate veterans in the General Assembly. They proposed a new institution and suggested that the institution be named in honor of General Stonewall Jackson. The act establishing the Stonewall Jackson Manual Training and Industrial School in Concord, North Carolina, became law on March 2, 1907. The act passed with all Confederate members voting in favor. The General Assembly collected $10,000 toward the project but was unable to buy a piece of land to build the school on. The board of trustees went to work with the communities. The citizens became interested in the project and joined in. They raised another $10,000 to buy a 293-acre piece of land in Cabarrus County. A generous donation from the King's Daughters and the North Carolina Federation of Women's Clubs of $5,000 enabled two cottages to be built on the property. James Cook's wife got local businesses to donate furnishings and amenities for the two cottages. On January 12, 1909, the school was complete. It housed the first students and staff in the new King's Daughters cottages. Over the next three decades, with state funds and private donations, the school built seventeen cottages.

There are rumors of what happened behind closed doors at the Stonewall Jackson Training School. There were stories of abuse and severe cruelty and rumors of being severely beaten and locked in closets for hours. There were stories of physical and mental abuse surrounding the school. Those who tried to escape would be caught, and the punishment would be much worse violence. Stories surrounding the school told that after World War II, there were six sterilizations performed on young boys.

A young boy named Daniel was fifteen in 1947 at the time he was sentenced to the Stonewall Jackson Training School for the first-degree murder of his father; he was to remain there until he was eighteen. Had he not killed his father, his mother surely would have died at his father's hands that night.

While serving his sentence, Daniel fell in love with Ellie Blum, daughter of the school's administrator. Ellie would volunteer to close the entrance gates in the evening so she could slip away and see Daniel. After closing the gate, Ellie would make her way to the chapel. Daniel's job was to clean and lock the chapel.

Under a full moon on a very foggy night in 1950, the young couple began their nightly trip. Daniel was on the bridge as he waited for Ellie. Ellie had to cross the road to get to the bridge. As she stepped out into the road, Daniel heard the roar of an engine and the screeching of tires heading in the direction of Ellie. He jumped off the bridge to go warn Ellie. When Daniel landed, he broke his ankle. He was unable to save her. For the past sixty-five years, whenever there's a full moon on a foggy night, you can see Daniel and Ellie on their nightly journey. There is no mention of Daniel dying in school records.

Unfortunately, since the Stonewall Jackson Training School closed, there has been little interest in preserving these historic buildings. In several buildings, the floors have caved in and the ceiling is falling down. Nature is slowing reclaiming the buildings.

You cannot visit the ruins of the Stonewall Jackson Training School. There are "no trespassing" signs all over the grounds, and the police make regular patrols in the area. The school is in the National Register of Historic Places.

Mermaid Point

Most legends in North Carolina involve ghostly visitors, monsters, UFOs and other haunting things. There is one legend in Chatham County that doesn't belong to any of these categories, and it's not scary. It's the Legend of Mermaid Point. Mermaid legends have been around since seafaring people. Mermaids have been argued by nonbelievers as simple folklore. But some men of the sea are firm believers in mermaids.

You might think that mermaids are only seen in the ocean, but according to legend, dating back to the 1700s, mermaids could be seen moon bathing and washing the salt water out of their hair in the Cape Fear River. There's a magical place called Mermaid Point where mermaids have been spotted sitting on a sandbar. The mermaids' favorite place was at the intersection of the Deep River and the Haw River at the headwater of the Cape Fear. The Cape Fear River runs all the way to the Atlantic Ocean.

In 1740, four men from Argyllshire, Scotland—Duncan Campbell, James McLachlan and Hector and Neill McNeill—bought large tracts of land where the Haw River and the Deep River merge. Together, they formed a town called Lockville. Ambrose Ramsey opened a tavern in the town. Ramsey's tavern sat right by the banks of the Deep River, a short distance from where it joined the Haw River. Ramsey was a Patriot in the Revolutionary War and a member of North Carolina's General Assembly. The tavern was involved in several battles in the Revolution.

Mermaid Point was near the tavern. In the wee hours of the morning, the tavern's patrons making their way home had to pass right by Mermaid Point.

That's where some eyewitness accounts came from. The legend says that the mermaids would appear around 2:00 a.m. The patrons of the tavern were quite gassed up when they left. Were the mermaids swimming all the way up from the Atlantic Ocean to see the gassed-up patrons, or were the patrons' wild imaginations making them see the mermaids? The observers said that if approached the mermaids, they would jump back into the river and disappear.

In the 1900s, the Buckhorn Dam was built and the entire area was flooded, washing away the tavern and the mermaids' sandbar. Another source says the tavern burned in the 1800s.

Bootlegger House

The historic Bootlegger House is an Eastlake house in the historic Fourth Ward of Charlotte. It was built in 1894. The house was originally on Caldwell Street in a neighborhood called Little Brooklyn. In the 1920s, during Prohibition, the house became a bootlegger headquarters. It got its name due to the hidden area under the foyer stairs behind the wainscoting, where illegal booze was hidden.

In the 1970s, the city planned to tear down the Bootlegger House to make way for the new government center. Michael Trent bought the house for fifty dollars and had it moved to its current location on North Poplar Street. The house has been restored and renovated and retains all of its original molding, mantels, heart pine floors and most of the pine siding.

In 1999, a man named John bought the Bootlegger House. After he moved in, he found wet footprints in the middle of the stairway. A few nights later, at 3:00 a.m., the water in the bathroom came on by itself. John turned it off. The next night, it came on again. John cut it off again. The water continued to come on for five nights in a row. Another bathroom was added in the downstairs part of the house. One day, the downstairs bathroom door was closed, and when John pulled it, it was locked from the inside. That particular lock could only be locked from the inside. The following morning, John was going to break the window to get in, but when he checked the door, it was unlocked.

Once, John went into the dining room and saw a chair balanced on two legs. The chair was not leaning against anything. John had recently gotten a blow torch to use for making crème brûlée. He kept the torch in a cabinet. When John went to get the torch, he found that it was lit. Another strange thing happened in the kitchen while John was cooking. He caught a glimpse of a man wearing a raincoat and hat. He shouted at the man, "OK, what do you want?" At that moment, a copper pot fell off the rack. John has also heard mysterious footsteps in the house when he was alone.

The house is thought to be haunted by the original owner, and he is said to be a mischievous ghost.

Just a Thought

Great disasters have taken place throughout recorded history. Some disasters are caused by human intervention and some by human negligence. From the time of Noah and the biblical flood and likely long before, natural disasters have been happening and will continue until the end of time. Natural and human-caused disasters are on the rise at an alarming rate. Revelations 6:12–13: "I looked when He opened the sixth seal and behold there was a great earthquake. And the stars of Heaven fell to the earth." Revelations 10:13: "In the same hour there was a great earthquake and a tenth of the city fell. In the earthquake 7,000 people were killed." Is the Maker trying to tell us something?

A *New York Times* article said that humanity has an extraordinary talent for causing catastrophes. We are even likely, as many have suggested over the past century, to be responsible for the coming apocalypse.

Natural disasters are sudden and extreme, caused by environmental factors such as earthquakes, volcanic eruptions, tornadoes, hurricanes and floods.

Human-caused disasters include train wrecks, fires, plane crashes and explosions. Most human-caused disasters are caused by human error. On April 15, 1912, the RMS *Titanic*, a British passenger liner, sank in the North Atlantic Ocean after colliding with an iceberg, resulting in the deaths of fifteen hundred passengers and crew. On February 1, 2003, the space shuttle *Columbia* broke apart while reentering the atmosphere over Texas, killing all seven crew.

Webster's New World Dictionary defines *disaster* as "an event causing great harm or damage."

Can the increase in natural disasters be a warning of things to come? What comes next? How will we handle it?

1906 Hamlet Train Wreck

On the hot summer day of July 22, 1906, at around 7:30 p.m., Seaboard Air Line passenger train no. 44 collided with a fruit train. The freight train carrying the fruit was westbound. The passenger train left Charlotte at 5:00 p.m. and was traveling at forty miles per hour. The two-train wreck was believed to be caused by a misunderstanding of orders or a lap order. The lap order meant the passenger train had orders to meet the freight train at Hamlet, North Carolina. The freight train orders were to meet the passenger train at Rockingham.

1906 Hamlet Train Wreck

The collision occurred about one mile from Hamlet in a deep cut. The accident was a head-on collision between the two trains when the freight train rounded a curve. The coach for the black passengers was completely destroyed, killing everyone onboard.

Both locomotives were destroyed, along with the baggage car and coaches. The tracks were piled high with wreckage from the two trains. Both first- and second-class coaches were overturned. The lamps in the passenger coaches were extinguished during the wreck, thus preventing a fire.

Railroad men, local citizens and the uninjured worked to recover the dead and get the injured out of the crumpled mess and to a hospital. There were twenty killed and forty-one injured.

1911 Hamlet Train Wreck

At 10:40 a.m. on July 27, 1911, one of the most disastrous train wrecks to ever happen on the Seaboard Air Line Railroad happened in front of the Hamlet roundhouse. In charge of train no. 33 were conductor William Bowen and engine man Ben Koonce. The train was carrying 912 passengers.

Train no. 33 was an African American excursion run by the St. Joseph's Sunday school in Durham, North Carolina. It left Durham and was headed to Charlotte when the head-on collision occurred with a freight train from Wilmington, North Carolina, that was coming into the yard. In charge of the freight train were engineer Archie Taylor and conductor Benton Brown. Both trains heading into the yard thought the track was clear.

The impact of the two-train head-on collision was heard all over town. The whistles from the roundhouse brought many Hamlet residents to the scene. The wreck destroyed six cars and both engines. The fourth and fifth cars were crumpled like pasteboard.

The uninjured and bystanders assisted in rescuing the injured and trapped. The dead were removed to a makeshift morgue in the carpenter shop. The car seats were put on the ground under the repair shed and used as a field hospital. Drs. Kinsman and Fowlkes from Hamlet, four doctors from Rockingham and several from Laurenburg and Aberdeen arrived on the scene to render as much medical assistance as possible under the trying conditions. Mrs. Landrum, a nurse from Presbyterian Hospital in

Charlotte, volunteered her services. A train was made up, and the injured were sent to the Good Samaritan Hospital and Mercy General Hospital in Charlotte.

The property loss to Seaboard was estimated at around $80,000. No one was blamed for the accident. There were eight dead, sixty seriously injured and twenty-eight with minor injuries.

1907 Eufola Train Wreck

On Sunday, July 1, 1907, at around 10:00 a.m., an eastbound freight train on the Western track had nine freight cars break loose and derail. The train was pulling twenty cars. A number of the cars were loaded with cattle and sheep. There were three cars carrying poultry. In charge of the train were engineer Roby and conductor Henry Tomlin. Mr. Bible and C.E. Brook were in charge of the poultry and cattle cars.

The derailment happened about nine miles west of Statesville and a quarter of a mile east of the Catawba River. The nine cars left the track as the train was crossing a fill. Four of the nine derailed cars were completely destroyed. The other five derailed cars left the track but did not overturn. A poultry car was the first to leave the track, and the other three cars piled on top of it. About five thousand chickens, ducks and turkeys were killed in the accident.

The engine and the first four cars traveled a short distance before they could stop. The caboose and other six cars that remained on the track soon stopped.

The engine and the four attached cars preceded to Eufola, about half a mile away, to drop the cars and report the accident. The engine then returned to the scene of the accident. The trainmen and section hands began at once to clear the track and make any necessary repairs. Passenger train no. 36 arrived shortly and picked up the passengers.

The news of the wreck spread at lightning speed. People began showing up from everywhere. As the crowd of spectators watched the thousands of chickens, ducks and turkeys running around in the wild, some decided to help themselves with a few and take them home for dinner. Some of the ducks made it to the river and disappeared.

In the late afternoon, a wrecking train arrived with a derrick and empty poultry cars. Some of the poultry was caught, and the tracks were cleared and opened before dark.

The cause of the wreck was not determined.

1908 Bessemer City Train Wreck

At 8:30 p.m. on a Sunday evening in August 1908, the New Orleans–New York limited train no. 38 met with an accident. The accident was one mile south of Bessemer City, North Carolina. Train traffic on the Charlotte Atlanta Division of the Southern Railway was halted for some time due to the train accident.

The tender and one postal car jumped the track and fell down a thirty-foot embankment. The locomotive remained on the track. One postal car, the club car, the diner car and part of one sleeper were derailed but did not overturn. The tracks were torn up for some distance.

The engineer, fireman and passengers were not injured. Five postal clerks—E.W. Hortt, Thomas McRae, T.L. Dean, L.H. Bowlin and C.B. White—were injured in the accident, but none fatally.

Wrecking trains and doctors were sent from Greenville and Spencer to the accident.

The cause of the train wreck is unknown.

1880 Charlotte Train Wreck

On December 27, 1880, two freight trains left Charlotte in sections. The first freight train left about fifteen minutes ahead of the other. The two trains were traveling on the Seaboard Air Line Railroad. The first train was under engineer Anthony. Engineer Wisenberry was in charge of the second.

On the upgrade just beyond the Paw Creek trestle, fourteen cars broke loose and stopped. In the rear car were flagman Robert Griffith and six passengers. Flagman Griffith warned the passengers on the stopped train about the danger. He started back down the track to signal the oncoming train but had not gotten very far when he heard the approaching train's whistle. Flagman Griffith could not go any farther down the track because of the 150-yard-long trestle. He began waving the flag as the engine came into view. As soon as engineer Wisenberry saw the flagman, he began putting on the brakes, but it was impossible to stop the heavy train as it was nearing the bottom of one of the steepest grades on the track. Before crossing the trestle, Wisenberry put the engine in reverse. At about 7:00 a.m., the trains collided. At the impact, Wisenberry was knocked down by a piece of firewood. The rear of the tender was thrown to one side, diverting the full impact of the train from the engine to the side of the cut where the cars were piled up. The stopped cars piled up in one large heap and caught fire. There was one injured and four killed.

1909 Reedy Fork Train Wreck

On December 15, 1909, passenger train no. 11, also known as the Richmond and Atlantic train, was traveling on the Southern Railway. At 6:32 a.m., the train derailed and wrecked at the Reedy Fork trestle. The train was carrying two baggage cars, an express car, several mail cars, three day coaches and two Pullmans.

The derailment was caused by a broken rail about two hundred feet from the trestle. The right rail was broken about eighteen inches from the joint. The rail was broken into many pieces for several feet and completely torn from the cross tie.

The engine, baggage, mail and express cars passed over the broken rail without any problem. The wheels of the day coaches went over the damaged rail, allowing the axles to fall on the guard rails of the bridge. The last five coaches went off the trestle and fell about thirty feet into the water below the trestle.

Most of those injured and killed were in the sleeper car, the Richmond. The Norfolk sleeper was also damaged. There were twelve dead and twenty-five injured. By 5:00 p.m., the tracks had been cleared, but there were still three cars in the water.

1884 Salisbury Train Wreck

In the early morning of August 20, 1884, freight train no. 19 left Charlotte in two sections. Captain A.B. White was the conductor on the section that left ten minutes ahead of the other section, and Captain Albright was the conductor on the second section.

Conductor Albright and engineer Smith from section two left their train to get breakfast. The fireman was put in charge until the return of the conductor and engineer. The pay train was in the area, and the fireman left the engine to go get his pay.

No one knew that while the engine had been waiting, the valves had been leaking. The cylinders were filling up with steam. When enough steam had built up in the cylinders, the wheels started to turn. As the train slowly moved, the valves continued to open until the train was traveling at full speed. When the fireman returned, the train was disappearing into the distance. Section two was made up of the engine and four cars.

Section one had just reached the water tank just beyond the Yadkin River Bridge and was preparing to take on water. Conductor White was working in the caboose when suddenly the horrible thundering sound of a runaway train broke the otherwise stillness of the day. Before conductor White could take any action or remove himself from the caboose, the runaway train tore through with a mighty force, smashing the car into tiny pieces leaving nothing resembling a caboose. The runaway train was traveling at about fifty miles an hour when the two trains impacted.

The crew of section one immediately began working to free the conductor. With conductor White's quick thinking, he managed to survive the horrendous crash. He was seriously injured and transported to a medical facility in Salisbury.

Witnesses say the runaway train was the fastest train they ever saw go over Yadkin Bridge.

The wrecked engine was returned to Salisbury and the track cleared as soon as possible to prevent delays from other trains.

1889 Mizpah Train Wreck

On the cold winter night of January 28, 1889, at around 9:00 p.m., northbound freight train no. 109 wrecked at a siding at Mizpah, North Carolina. The 109 left Charlotte pulling thirty-five cars.

The accident took place where the north- and southbound trains meet, at what railroad men call a spur. It is a piece of track where the northbound train can pull off so the southbound train can safely pass by. It can only be entered by the northbound train.

The siding ends abruptly on the trestle over the creek. The train was approaching the siding and going downgrade at about thirty-five miles an hour. When the pilot wheels hit the switch, the engine jerked to the right, moving forward on the spur. The engineer, realizing something wasn't right, called out for the crew to abandon the train as he was jumping from it. Before the crew realized what was going on, it was too late. For some reason, this time the switch was misplaced. When the engine reached the end of the siding, it continued on and plunged into the creek bed, carrying all fourteen cars with it.

Flames began to shoot up from the train wreckage. The crew could see the fireman was pinned down. They poured buckets of water on him to prevent him from being burned alive. Sydney Lee, the brakeman, was buried beneath the train and never found. His was the only death attributed to this accident. The Reidsville Fire Department arrived on the scene and put out the fire. The fireman was rescued at 5:00 a.m. on Sunday morning.

The inspectors believe the switch had been turned in order to intentionally wreck the train.

1965 Train and Pickup Collision

On July 10, 1965, a pickup truck loaded with two members of the Rock Hill Blue Devils (an Indian sand lot baseball team) and a group of spectators was struck by an Atlantic Coast Line railroad freight train as the pickup was trying to cross the railroad tracks ahead of the train. The accident occurred at a high banked rural crossing about two and a half miles southeast of Laurenburg, North Carolina. The two members of the ball team were killed. The other deaths were the spectators. The driver of the truck was the lone survivor. The rest of the team had gone on ahead in two cars.

Robeson County police said the truck just pulled in front of the oncoming train. Highway patrolman J.E. Powell said the truck was knocked about forty-five feet from where the impact occurred. The bodies were strewn between fifty and three hundred feet from the impact.

The train was pulling two cars and a caboose. There were no deaths on the train.

1925 Coal Glenn Mining Catastrophe

On May 27, 1925 at 9:30 a.m., an explosion at the Carolina Coal Company mine in the little mining town of Coal Glenn, Chatham County, North Carolina, rocked the countryside. The first explosion occurred in the second right lateral of the mine, about one thousand feet from the entrance. Two more explosions followed about thirty minutes apart and were believed to have happened between the second right shaft and the opening.

Mine records showed that fifty-nine men went into the mine at 8:00 a.m. After the explosion, mine officials reported that seventy-one miners' lamps were missing. At the time, mine officials believed that seventy-one men might represent the number of miners entombed in the mine.

Surrounding states rushed rescue workers to the mine. The American Legion Auxiliary and the Red Cross rushed in to assist where needed. Adjutant General Metts arrived late in the day and took charge on behalf of Governor McLean. Frank Page, chairman of the State Highway Commission, brought a corps of engineers to the mine. Miners from the Cumnock Company aided in the rescue. Sheriff G.W. Blair hastened to the mine and swore in twenty more deputies to help control the situation of the growing number of civilians gathering at the mine. Fort Bragg sent the Ambulance Corps. Dorsey J. Parker, chief engineer for the Pittsburgh Bureau of Miners, was in charge of the rescue work.

Bodies of the miners were taken eight miles to the Sanford, North Carolina undertaking establishment to identify and prepare for shipment to their burial locations.

Fifty-three miners died in the coal mine disaster.

Steamer *Olive* Struck by Tornado

On February 17, 1903, at around 11:00 a.m., the passenger ship *Olive*, a single-screw steamboat owned by J.A. Pertlow of Franklin, Virginia, left that city. At 9:00 p.m., the passenger ship passed Hollies Wharf. The *Olive* was navigating the Chowan River in North Carolina between Mount Pleasant and Oliver's Wharf. The *Olive* had been making regular trips between Virginia and North Carolina for several years.

The weather was continuing to decline and finally became so fierce that Captain Withy turned the *Olive* around to return up the river for safety. At 2:00 a.m., everything became inky black. There was no light except the lights on the *Olive*. There was no visibility. A terrible roaring sound broke through the sound of the wind. Something struck the *Olive* on its port beam and turned the ship on its side. A tidal wave passed over the disabled ship and flooded the hold. In less than two minutes, the steamboat *Olive* was resting on the bottom of the Chowan River. The pilot house was the only part to remain above water.

Most of the passengers and crew were below and had no chance of escape. Captain George H. Withy and five others survived standing in waist-deep water in the pilot house until 6:00 a.m. in the morning when a Norfolk and Southern steamer rescued them. They were let off at Edenton.

Engineer Conway, assistant J.P. Murphy, J.N. Bell and five other unnamed persons left on a lifeboat. Those in the lifeboat were picked up several hours later by the tugboat *Gazelle* of the John L. Roper Lumber Company. They were dropped off at Tunis.

Steamer Olive
Struck By Tornado

Eighteen people died in the accident.

Five years before the weather caused this accident, the steamer sprang a leak and went down within sight of this disaster.

The *Olive* was an inland passenger steamer from Norfolk, Virginia. It was built in 1869, weighing 287 tons, 120 feet 9 inches long, with a beam of 20 feet 4 inches and a hold depth of 7 feet.

1957 Fort Bragg Lightning Strike

On June 19, 1957, a severe thunderstorm moved across Fort Bragg, North Carolina, between 5:00 and 6:00 p.m., bringing lightning bolts from the electrical storm that struck Fort Bragg bivouac troops. Within a ten-minute period, lightning struck twice, killing two National Guardsmen and injuring forty-seven others.

Units from the Tenth Old Hickory division of the North Carolina National Guard took the worst part of the severe weather. The guardsmen were camped in the woods for their summer training. They were about ten miles west of the main base. The lightning struck twice during suppertime, while many of the National Guardsmen were standing in line with their mess kits. Many of the guardsmen were knocked down like bowling pins. The primary damage was centered on the bivouac area.

Private First Class Truesdale's mess kit was knocked from his hand and bent out of shape by the force of the lightning strike. While the uninjured were trying to help the injured, another lightning bolt struck. The lightning bolt skipped around the bivouac area, injuring more National Guardsmen. The ground shook something terrible. Many of the guardsmen reported that their feet felt like the ground was burning up. Guardsmen were calling for the medic, who was also knocked down. One of the cooks was knocked out by the lightning bolt.

The base hospital called in off-duty medical personnel to assist with the forty-seven injured guardsmen. Four of the guardsmen were admitted to the hospital as patients. The others remained at the hospital overnight for observation.

More than three miles from the center of the storm, Captain Britt was on a field phone when an electrical jolt threw him across a tent. Lieutenant Colonel Hillebrand was miles away when his right eye was injured because he received a shock through a telephone receiver.

1936 Greensboro Tornadoes

On April 1 and 2, 1936, Greensboro, North Carolina, saw twelve tornadoes in a fourteen-hour period. The tornado outbreak was caused by a super cell storm system. The tornadoes caused great destruction across North Carolina. Some tornadoes reached an F4 on the Fujita scale. The tornadoes developed in three waves. These were the first recorded tornadoes in the history of Greensboro.

On April 2, the tornadoes that hit Greensboro left a path of F4 damage to the city. The south side of the city sustained most of the damage. One tornado touched down near High Point Road and Elm Street and continued east to the east of Bennett College. The tornado cut a path two and a half miles long and four blocks wide. The 400 block of Gorrell Street had only one building left on the foundation. The tornado passed within one mile north of Mebane, destroying three homes, killing one person and injuring five others. The tornadoes did $2 million in damage just in Greensboro and were responsible for 14 deaths and 144 injuries. This was the second-deadliest tornado in North Carolina history. In addition, 56 buildings were completely destroyed and 233 more were damaged. Crews armed with shovels, picks, axes and a few tractors dug through the ruins in search of survivors. More disasters were coming. Fires followed the tornadoes despite a downpour of rain.

Industrial plants were completely wiped out, including the Old El Moro cigar plant, the George C. Brown Lumber Company, the J.D. Wilkins Steelworks plant, the Red Band Flower plant, the Dillard Paper

Company, the Sinclair Refining Company and the Glasscock Stone and Manufacturing Company. The only thing left undamaged at the Sinclair plant was the storage tanks. The Blue Bell Overall Company was also damaged.

Forty-four deaths in North Carolina were attributed to the tornado outbreak.

1942 Smithfield Ammunition Truck Explosion

At 2:57 a.m. on Saturday, March 7, 1942, a massive explosion shook the countryside. A truck carrying thirty thousand pounds of black powder, grenades and other explosives to be delivered to the army collided with a car on Highway 301 south of Selma, North Carolina. The explosion happened about two hours after the wreck. Both vehicles caught on fire.

The explosion was seen and heard fifty miles away. The explosion blew a crater twenty feet deep in the highway and ripped a thirty-foot-wide trench in the cement highway. The Tarlton Hotel, Luke Capp's filling station and Gurkin's Tavern were completely destroyed from the blast. The only remains of Luke Capp's filling station were two crumpled-up gas pumps. Homes within a five-hundred-yard radius suffered severe damage. The town of Selma was one mile from the scene of the explosion and had all windows shattered. Selma Cotton Mill had nine hundred window panes broken. The town of Smithfield, three miles away, suffered broken windows. Parts of the ammunition truck were scattered across a one-and-a-half-mile area.

Six people were killed by the wreck or explosion, and over one hundred were injured. The most seriously injured were transported to hospitals in Johnston County, Goldsboro, Raleigh and Durham.

Fire departments responded from Selma and Smithfield but were unable to extinguish the fire due to the amount of black powder. Commander of the New Holland CCC camp George Stroupe and Cecil

E. Propst, game and fish warden at the camp, were killed when passing by the accident. Minnie Lewis, the driver of the car involved in the accident, later died from burns sustained in the accident. Two bodies were found in the smoking debris of the Talton Hotel, and another body was found near the hotel.

1942 Gas Tanker Collides with Passenger Bus

On October 3, 1942, in the predawn hours, a tragedy occurred. A gasoline tanker with a full load of gasoline traveling from Lumberton to Fort Bragg came up behind a wagon loaded with cotton. The wagon did not have any lights on it, and the tanker driver, unable to see it at a distance, had to swerve to miss a full impact with the wagon. The tanker slightly sideswiped the wagon and hit head-on a capacity-loaded Queen City Trailways bus, exploding on impact.

Many of the passengers on the bus were able to escape the burning bus with non–life threatening injuries. Eleven passengers died at the scene, and eighteen were injured. The eighteen injured were taken to the Lumberton Hospital. The bus driver died at the Baker Sanatorium. The wagon driver was only slightly hurt. The dead were taken to St. Pauls, a nearby village.

Smoke from the tanker and bus fire rose hundreds of feet into the air. The tanker and bus were reduced to a pile of charred steel.

1975 Siloam Road Bridge Collapse

On Sunday, February 23, 1975, at 9:25 p.m., during a heavy fog, a car struck a timber railing on the Siloam Road Bridge, causing the middle section of the bridge to collapse and fall thirty feet into the rain-swollen Yadkin River. The thick, heavy fog prevented the driver of the car from seeing the bridge timber.

The Siloam Road Bridge was a one-lane steel span bridge that connected Yadkin and Surry Counties near Siloam in northwestern North Carolina. The span of steel had a wooden floor and was about three hundred feet long. More than two hundred feet of the bridge was over water.

There were two cars on the bridge at the time of the collapse. Mr. and Mrs. Hugh Atkinson were in the first car that went down. The second car to fall landed on top of the Atkinsons' car, killing all in both vehicles.

The thick fog obscured the fallen bridge. Within a seventeen-minute period, six more vehicles drove off the bridge. Some of the vehicles fell on the Yadkin side, while others fell on the Surry side.

Eugene Livengood, a lone member of the Fall Creek Volunteer Fire Department, was the first on the scene, but the fog was so thick that he had to wait until a rescue unit arrived. Rescue units responded from Forsyth, Yadkin, Surry and Stokes Counties.

Four died in the bridge accident. One person who was rescued from the disaster would later become the Surry County sheriff, Graham Atkinson. At the time of the accident, he was ten years old. Ten others were hospitalized in good condition.

In the 1970s, state officials posted a sign on the bridge that read, "Local traffic only."

The Atkinson family found a letter in Hugh Atkinson's coat pocket that he had written to the governor's office urging action on the bridge. Weeks before the accident, Hugh had urged state officials to tear the bridge down.

According to an unconfirmed report, the bridge had been condemned several months before the accident but was resurfaced and okayed for use.

The bridge collapse attracted national attention to bridge safety. It was reported in a national *Reader's Digest* and was featured on the *CBS Evening News*.

Two Hydrogen Bombs Fall on North Carolina

On January 23 (another source says 24), 1961, bright orange flames lit up the sky over the town of Faro in Wayne County, North Carolina, only three days after the inauguration of President John F. Kennedy. With the fear of the Cold War on everyone's mind, American bombers were kept airborne at all times. The aircraft, a B-52 Stratofortress bomber, had been patrolling over the Atlantic Ocean. Twelve hours had passed since the B-52 left Seymour Johnson Air Force Base near Goldsboro, North Carolina, with a crew of eight. The bomber was carrying two 3.8-megaton Mark 39 hydrogen bombs. Each hydrogen bomb had 260 times the explosive power of the bomb dropped on Hiroshima, Japan. The B-52 was part of a fleet of twelve bombers in the air prepared to defend the United States against a Soviet attack.

Around midnight on January 23 or 24, the B-52 rendezvoused with an air tanker for an aerial refueling. During the refueling, the tanker notified the B-52 commander, Major Walter Tullock, that there was a fuel leak in the right wing. They aborted the refueling and notified ground control of the situation. Ground control directed the B-52 to assume a holding pattern off the coast until most of the fuel had been used. Fuel started to pour out of the wing. Nineteen tons were dropped in two minutes. Ground control directed the B-52 to return to Seymour Johnson Air Force Base.

The pilot made an unsuccessful attempt to get back to the base. At ten thousand feet, the right wing broke off the plane. The pilot ordered

Two Hydrogen Bombs fall on North Carolina

the crew to jump. At nine thousand feet, five crewmen jumped into the darkness and safely landed. The sixth man jumped but didn't survive. The plane went into a spin and a nosedive straight down to earth. Two died in the crash.

Witnesses reported the plane explosion looked like daylight. Other witnesses compared it to a roman candle. A farmer saw his fields light up with fireballs. Some of the locals thought that Armageddon had come. None of the locals knew what had happened. The debris field was north of Musgrave's Crossroads near Faro and Eureka, fifteen miles from Goldsboro.

The two hydrogen bombs broke loose and plunged to the ground. One of the hydrogen bombs landed in a field with its parachute tangled in the tree limbs. The second bomb didn't land so softly. It was entombed in the ground after falling at seven hundred miles per hour. Each bomb carried a payload of four megatons, the equivalent of four million tons of TNT.

When Earl Lancaster, Faro Volunteer Fire Department assistant chief, arrived on the scene, everything was burning. Within the hour, military helicopters were in the area. Military officials evacuated everyone in the area.

The military kept it secret just how close the accident came to causing a nuclear catastrophe of biblical proportions. The air force reported that at no time was there any chance of a nuclear explosion.

A secret document published in declassified form by the *Guardian* revealed another side of the story. The document, obtained by investigative journalist Eric Schlosser under the Freedom of Information Act, gave conclusive evidence that the United States narrowly escaped a nuclear disaster of monumental proportions. One simple Dynamo-Technology low-voltage switch stood between a safe fall and a catastrophe of epic proportions. All four of the safety mechanisms worked perfectly on one of the bombs, but three failed to work on the other one.

If one of the bombs had exploded, lethal fallout could have gone as far as Washington, D.C.; Baltimore, Maryland; Philadelphia, Pennsylvania; and New York City. It would have killed everything within an eight-and-a-half-mile radius.

When the government was trying to recover the bomb that was buried, it continuously ran into water problems. As workers dug the hole deeper, it continued to fill up. They continued to pump out the water but were unsuccessful at recovering the entire buried bomb.

The military purchased an easement from Davis (only name given) and his heirs. The agreement states "that no current or future land owner may dig or drill deeper than five feet or use the land in any manner other than growing crops, timber or pasture land." The government still collects samples from wells near the crash.

The official report from the Pentagon states that "pieces of the bomb that crashed into the swamp broke off. One of those pieces was never found."

Dr. Jack Revelle was the officer who deactivated the bombs at the crash site.

Air Midwest Flight 5481 Crash

On January 8, 2003, at 8:47:28 a.m. Eastern Standard Time, Air Midwest, doing business as US Airways Express flight 5481, crashed shortly after takeoff from runway 18R at Charlotte Douglas International Airport. The NTSB (National Transportation Safety Board) said flight 5481 was a regularly scheduled passenger flight to Greenville-Spartanburg International Airport in South Carolina.

Visual meteorological conditions prevailed at the time of the crash. The plane crashed thirty-seven seconds into the flight. The passenger plane was completely destroyed by the impact and post-crash fire.

The plane was a Raytheon Beechcraft 1900D, 2N233YV. It was operating under the provisions of 14 code of the federal regulations part 121 on an instrument flight rules flight plan.

The plane crashed into a US Airways maintenance hangar on CLT property and came to rest about 1,600 feet beyond the runway 18R threshold. ATCT (air traffic control tower) controllers heard an emergency locater transmitter signal beginning at 8:47:29:10 a.m.

The investigators determined the cause of the crash was the result of two different issues. After takeoff, the plane climbed steeply even though both pilots were pushing the control column forward. The plane was not responding and stalled, leading to the crash. The turn buckles controlling tension on the elevators had been incorrectly set. The pilots did not have sufficient pitch control.

Two flight crew and nineteen passengers aboard were killed. One person on the ground received minor injuries.

1994 US Air Flight 1016 Crash

On Saturday, July 2, 1994, US Air flight 1016, a McDonnell Douglas DC9, departed Columbia Metropolitan Airport in South Carolina at 6:15 p.m. The flight was scheduled for thirty-five minutes to Charlotte/Douglas International Airport. There were fifty-two passengers, three flight attendants and two pilots aboard.

It started off as an uneventful flight for the DC9 until the approach to Charlotte/Douglas International Airport. There were several severe thunderstorms in the immediate vicinity of the airport, which made landing difficult. Flight 1016 was cleared to land on runway 18R. The storms in the Charlotte area had reduced visibility to about one mile. On final approach, the pilot, realizing they were in trouble, instructed the first officer to take the plane around. The plane struggled to climb due to the weather conditions. The plane veered to the right and began a rapid descent. At 6:42 p.m., the plane crashed into a field on the Charlotte/Douglas International Airport property about a half mile from the runway. It broke through the airport fence, hit several trees and broke apart as it slid down a residential street near the airport. The front part of the plane came to rest on Wallace Neal Road. The rear section came to rest in the carport of a nearby residence.

Thirty-seven passengers died, fourteen had serious injuries and one had minor injuries. Several of the flight crew suffered serious injuries. There were no crew deaths, and no one on the ground was injured.

The NTSB concluded that a microburst generated by the severe thunderstorm contributed to the crash. The meteorological phenomenon known as a microburst is a downdraft or sinking air in a thunderstorm. There are two types of microburst, a wet and a dry. A wet microburst occurs within the rain shaft of a thunderstorm. A dry microburst will not have any rain associated with it. They usually occur in dry thunderstorms or ahead of a thunderstorm.

1954 Transport Plane Crashes

Shortly after 10:00 a.m. on March 30, 1954, a crippled C119 Flying Boxcar troop carrier was attempting to make an emergency landing on the parade ground at Fort Bragg, North Carolina. As it was attempting to land, the Flying Boxcar was leaning badly from a burning engine. The pilot, unable to control the plane as it went down, hit the top of the officers' barracks and skidded across the parade ground and into the mess hall. The plane exploded into flames along with the mess hall. Soldiers rushed to the scene and pulled three men from the rear section of the plane.

The crash killed seven men and injured ten others. Four men from the plane escaped and were sent to the hospital. Airman 1C Eugene R. Snyder, twenty-three, was the flight engineer and the only man to walk away from the crash.

It took firemen almost two hours to bring the fire under control. One rescue worker was injured when he was sprayed with flames when a gas tank exploded.

1960 Planes Collide Near Hickory

A private twin-engine Cessna 310 owned by the Bergsma Brothers Furniture Company of Grand Rapids, Michigan, collided with a Piedmont Airlines F-27 turboprop on Wednesday, April 20 or 21,

1960. The two planes were operating under visual flight rules while making their landing approach at the Hickory, North Carolina airport. The airport didn't have a control tower.

A witness to the accident said the Cessna flew in front of the Piedmont airliner and hit the airliner's left wing, damaging it. The Cessna 310 disintegrated as it dropped straight down about one thousand feet to the ground. The two planes were about three hundred yards from the landing strip. With no serious damage, the Piedmont airliner continued on and made a safe landing without any injuries to the thirty-six passengers and four crew members.

The Cessna was carrying three passengers and one pilot. Their lifeless bodies were found in the fuselage. The wreckage was scattered in a one-hundred-yard circle on Forrest Gaines's farm.

1974 Eastern Airlines Jet Crash

On Wednesday, September 11, 1974, at 7:00 a.m., Eastern Airlines flight 212 departed Charleston, South Carolina, with a stopover in Charlotte before continuing on to Chicago. At 7:34 a.m., the Eastern Airlines DC-9-31, flight 212, was attempting to make a landing at the fog-shrouded Douglas Municipal Airport in Charlotte. The plane was making an instrument landing using a straight-in-approach. It was traveling fifty knots too fast and five hundred feet below the final approach fix. On final approach, the plane flew in too low and struck the trees 3.3 miles short of the runway. The plane exploded after plummeting into a hillside, sending a fireball and black smoke hundreds of feet into the already foggy air. Rescue workers found bodies scattered hundreds of yards from the crash site.

There were seventy-eight passengers and four crew members on board. Sixty-eight passengers and two crew members were killed in the crash. Another source said seventy-two died.

It was considered a miracle that anyone survived the crash. Thirty-eight passengers with ties to Charleston were on board.

Both plane recorders were recovered. The cause of the crash was ruled pilot error. Jim Ashlock, public relations director of the Miami Eastern Airlines, said, "Mystery surrounded the crash. The plane had been given clearance to land just moments before it plummeted into the hillside."

A makeshift morgue was set up at the National Guard Armory near the airport. The bodies arrived in refrigerated trucks. The FBI was in charge of identifying the victims.

1961 Jet Bomber Crash Near Denton

At 9:15 p.m. on March 30, 1961, a U.S. Air Force Boeing B-52G Stratofortress Atomic Bomber exploded and crashed at Silver Hill Road four miles from the Davidson County town of Denton, North Carolina. The B-52G jet was on a routine mission from Dow Air Force Base in Maine and lost control during an aerial refueling attempt. The B-52G was in the observation position one to two hundred feet behind and below the tanker plane.

The B-52G mysteriously exploded in midair. The remains of the plane crashed to earth, creating another massive explosion. The second explosion shook the town of Denton and could be seen as far away as Winston-Salem, North Carolina. Windows in homes and businesses were blown out, woods and fields in the crash area caught fire and debris from the plane was scattered across a ten-mile radius.

Military personnel from Seymour-Johnson Air Force Base in Goldsboro, North Carolina, along with local rescue workers, conducted the cleanup and search for missing bodies. Fire departments and rescue squads from Thomasville, Forsyth County, Randolph County, Davidson County and Guilford County responded to the scene. Helicopters came from as far away as Elizabeth City to help search for missing crewmen. Parts of the crewmen's bodies were found a mile and a half away from the crash site. Only two crewmen survived, Major Wilber F. Minnich and First Lieutenant Glen C. Franham. Six men died as a result of the crash. The two survivors were treated for minor injuries at Denton's Griffis Clinic.

Fifty years later, a large crater remains in the woods off Silver Hill Road. Pieces of the plane can still be found in the area—a grim reminder of what happened that night. The plane crashed several hundred yards away from John Frank's home on the border between Frank's farm and a farm owned by N.L. Lookabill. Trees were ripped up by the roots for hundreds of feet around the crater. The crater measured 150 feet in length, 50 feet wide at its widest point and 25 to 40 feet deep.

1994 Green Ramp Disaster

In the early morning of Wednesday, March 23, 1994, shortly after 2:00 a.m., a twin-seat F-16D fighter from the Seventy-Fourth Fighter Squadron, Twenty-Third Operations Group, collided with a C-130E Hercules transport from the Second Airlift Squadron 317 Group Pope Air Force Base. Both aircraft were members of the Twenty-Third Wing. The F-16D, with two pilots on board, was conducting a simulated flameout (SFO) approach. Both pilots thought they were cleared to land. At three hundred feet above Pope Air Force Base, the two planes collided. The nose of the F-16D severed the C-130's right elevator. When the two planes collided, the pilot in the F-16D applied full afterburner in an attempt to recover the plane, but the plane had already begun to disintegrate. Debris from the F-16D began to shower the approaching runway. The pilot was unable to stabilize the plane. He and the other pilot ejected. The C-130 flew away from the airfield to check to see if it could land safely. Meanwhile, the F-16D, still on full afterburner, continued on toward Green Ramp, the large north–south parking ramp at the west end of Pope Air Force Base's east–west runway. The F-16D hit Green Ramp heading west. The F-16D was traveling about 180 miles per hour on impact. The C-130 landed safely with no injuries.

Flying metal from the F-16D punctured the fuel tanks on a C-141 transport plane preparing for takeoff. The C-141 was destroyed in a sudden blaze from the ruptured fuel tank. The six C-141 crewmen escaped without injury.

On the day of the crash, five hundred paratroopers from Fort Bragg, North Carolina, were in the Pax shed on the Green Ramp. The remains of the F-16D slid into the staging area where the paratroopers were. At the scene, paratroopers were pulling fellow paratroopers from the flames of the burning plane and the exploding 20 mm ammunition from the F-16D.

Responding medical units came from the army Delta Force and a number of U.S. Army tactical ambulances with medical teams from the Fifty-Fifth Medical Group. The injured were transported to Womack Army Medical Center at Fort Bragg and the U.S. Army Institute of Surgical Research at Brooke Medical Center in Texas.

President Clinton visited the crash site two days later and visited the injured at Womack and Fort Bragg.

West Pharmaceutical Services Explosion

On a Wednesday afternoon, January 29, 2003, an industrial disaster of epic proportion occurred when a pharmaceutical plant in Kingston, North Carolina, experienced an explosion. The explosion ripped through the plant, leaving it in ruins. Half of the plant was destroyed by the explosion and fire. Debris from the two eight-hundred-foot-high water tanks flew into the air seconds after the blast. Damage to the plant was estimated at $150 million.

The explosion occurred in the four-story area where chemicals were mixed. A chain reaction of explosions rapidly propagated, leaving the plant in ruins. The fire raged for two days, sending columns of black acrid smoke into the air. The shockwaves shattered windows up to one thousand feet away. Burning debris was thrown two miles, starting forest fires. The explosion was felt twenty-five miles away.

WRAL TV reported that at least 3 people had been killed and 37 injured. About 130 people were working in the plant when the explosion occurred. The injured were treated at the North Carolina Jaycee Burn Center in Chapel Hill, Lenoir Memorial Hospital in Kingston, Pitt Memorial Hospital and Duke Medical Center in Durham and Wayne Memorial Hospital in Goldsboro, North Carolina.

The Kingston Fire Department responded first. The first emergency crews to arrive on the scene were rescuing employees who were dangling from the steel beams in the rear of the building. The Red Cross set up a family service center at Immanuel Baptist Church.

Residents within one mile of the plant were urged to evacuate by the Lenoir County Emergency Communications due to the acrid smoke and fumes of burning plastic.

THE INVESTIGATION

The investigation focused on two possibilities: the failure of a newly installed gas line or a large dust explosion. The Chemical Safety and Hazard Investigations Board determined that the explosion originated in the area known as the automated compounding system. The working theory was that it was a rubber dust explosion. The investigation determined that something disturbed the dust, creating a dust cloud that ignited.

Sources

Television

A&E Television Network
The History Channel
WBTV 13 Charlotte

Magazines

Cryptozoology News.
Dunn, Mark. *Style Blueprint* [Charlotte].
Goss, Mary. *Charlotte Agenda*, October 24, 2018.
Inscoe, Corey. *Charlotte Five*, October 30, 2015.
Our State, August 2012.
Schaefer, Cindy. *Raleigh Magazine*, September 24, 2015.

Books and Journals

American Journal of Science and Arts 9, no. 2.
Barrett, John G. *The Civil War in North Carolina*. N.p., 1963.
Bradley, Mark L. *Last Stand in the Carolinas: The Battle of Bentonville*. N.p., 1996.
Brown, Alan. *Haunted South*. Charleston, SC: The History Press, 2014.

Casstevens, Frances H. *Ghosts of the North Carolina Piedmont*. Charleston, SC: The History Press, 2009.

Chowan College. *Chowanoka*. Repr., 1914.

Encyclopedia of North Carolina. N.p., n.d.

Faulkner, Ronnie W. *Battle of Bentonville*. N.p., 2006.

Fitzhugh, Pat. *Ghostly Cries from Dixie*. N.p.: Armand Press, 2009.

Guiley, R.E. *Encyclopedia of Ghosts and Spirits*. N.p.: Roundhouse Publishing Ltd., 1992.

Journal of the Elisha Mitchell Scientific Society 1 (1884).

Maxwell, Tom. "For the Scrutiny of Science and the Light of Revelation." *Southern Cultures*, Spring 2012.

Newman, Rich. *Haunted Bridges*. Woodbury, MN: Llewellyn Publications, 2016.

Pennington-Hopkins, Vivian. *Gold Hill Ghosts and Other Legends*. N.p., 2009.

Roberts, Nancy. *Illustrated Guide to Ghosts*. N.p.: Castle Books, 1975.

Simms, William Gilmore. *Geography of South Carolina*. N.p., 1843.

Sterling, Roger Manley. *Weird Carolinas*. New York, 2007.

Thay, Edrick. *Ghost Stories of the Old South*. N.p.: Ghost House Books, 2003.

Zepke, Terrance. *Best Ghost Tales of North Carolina*. Sarasota, FL: Pineapple Press, 2011.

Newspapers

Aiken Standard, July 3, 1994.

Aiken Standard and Review, March 31, 1954.

Associated Press, May 28, 1925.

Atlanta Constitution, August 21, 1884.

———, February 18, 1903.

———, January 29, 1889.

Attride, Tiana. *Daily Tarheel*, October 7, 2015.

Bennett, Abbie, and Josh Shaffer. *Raleigh News and Observer*, January 11, 2018.

Biloxi Daily Herald, August 4, 1908.

Bordsen, John. *Charlotte Observer*, October 3, 2014.

Burlington Daily Times, June 20, 1957.

Burlington Daily Times-News, April 3, 1936.

———, February 24, 1975.

Charleston Post and Courier, September 11, 2009.

Charlotte Daily Observer, July 23, 1906.

————, July 28, 1911.

————, March 10, 1876.

Charlotte Democrat, April 18, 1884.

————, April 25, 1884.

Chatham Record, April 24, 1884.

————, June 4, 1925.

Columbus Enquirer-Sun, July 24, 1906.

Daily Mail Reporter, July 28, 2013.

Durham Herald Sun, n.d.

Fayetteville Observer, October 31, 1998.

————, October 31, 2018.

Fayetteville Observer-Times, March 24, 1994.

Feltman, Rachel. *Washington Post*, n.d.

Florence Morning News, October 4, 1942.

————, September 12, 1974.

Greensboro Patriot, April 24, 1884.

Greenville News, n.d.

High Point Enterprise, March 31, 1961.

Ingle, Ivy. *Daily Tarheel*, October 19, 2016.

Kingsport News, April 21, 1960.

Mason City Globe Gazette, March 7, 1942.

Morning Herald, May 28, 1925.

Neal, Dale. *Asheville Citizen-Times*, March 14, 2015.

New York Daily News, December 26, 2015.

New York Times, December 28, 1880.

————, February 18, 1903.

————, May 28, 1925.

Olean Evening Herald, May 28, 1925.

Panama City Herald, June 20, 1957.

Pattison, Kate. *Raleigh Commons*, April 27, 2009.

Portillo, Ely. *Charlotte Observer*, March 23, 2017.

Price, Mark. *Charlotte Observer*, April 17, 2018.

————. *Charlotte Observer*, August 10, 2017.

Progress Clear Field, March 24, 1994.

Progress-Index, July 7, 1965.

Raleigh News and Observer, October 30, 2016.

Salt Lake Herald Republican, December 16, 1909.

San Mateo Times, June 20, 1957.

Shaffer, Josh. *Raleigh News and Observer*, February 28, 2018.

Sources

————. *Raleigh News and Observer*, November 7, 2017.
The State, August 3, 1908.
Statesville Landmark, August 27, 1891.
————, February 20, 1903.
Statesville Record and Landmark, n.d.
————, July 2, 1907.
Steelman, Ben. *Wilmington Star News*, January 20, 2018.
United Press.
United Press International.
Vann, Tap. *Weekly World News*, July 29, 2013.
Weekly Raleigh Register, April 23, 1884.
Wilson Advance, May 2, 1884.

Government

National Register of Historic Places, National Park Service
National Transportation Safety Board
United States National Museum

Science

Bryner, Jeanna. Live Science.
Hecket, Andrew. Appalachian State University professor.
Journal of Scientific Reports.
Nesbitt, Sterling. Virginia Polytechnic Institute.
Schneider, Vincent. North Carolina Museum of Natural Sciences.
Zanno, Lindsay, and Susan Drymala. North Carolina State University and the North Carolina Museum of Natural Sciences.

Websites

A

accuweather.com
airforce-togetherweserved.com
americanroadtrip.com

Sources

anomalist.com
aol.com
atlasobscura.com
aviation-safety.net
awwnews.com

B

blogs.lib.unc.edu
boards.ancestry.com
bootsnall.com

C

cabarrusmagazine.com
candidslice.com
carolinainn.com
catawbapioneer.com
charlotteagenda.com
charlottestories.com
chastynicole72.wordpress.com
chathamrabbit.blogspot.com
christianpost.com
city-data.com
cmhpf.org
cnn.com
courier-tribune.com
cryptidchronicles.tumblr.com
cryptidz.wikia.com

D

dalejyoung.com
deadmule.com
deepseanews.com
dictionary.com
doaliviart.wordpress.com
duke-energy.com

E

en.wikipedia.org
exploreyourspirits.com

F

facebook.com
facebook.com/carolinasunknown
files.usgwarchives.net
findagrave.com
freepages.history.rootsweb.ancestry.com

G

genealogybuff.com
geocaching.com
gimghoulcastle.blogspot.com
gradschool.unc.edu
greyareanews.com

H

hauntednc.com
hauntedplaces.org
haunted-places-to-go.com
hauntedrooms.com
hauntedstories.net
hauntin.gs
hauntworld.com
historicgoldhill.com
historichorrors.wordpress.com
historic-house.wikia.com
historicoakwoodcemetery.org
history.com
hubpages.com
hungamahub.com

J

jmpressley.net

K

kenyetothe.com

L

lavilo.com
libguides.chowan.edu
linkedpendium.com
livescience.com
loc.gov
loquisearch.com

M

mermaidpoint.com
meteorite-times.com
minsocam.org
mysteriousuniverse.org

N

nbcnews.com
ncdcr.gov
ncghostguide.byethost12.com
ncghoststories.blogspot.com
nchistoricsites.org
nchistorytoday.wordpress.com
nclegends.weebly.com
ncmarkers.com
ncpedia.org
ncsmalltown.com
news.ncsu.edu
947smoke.com
northcarolinaghosts.com

northcarolinaroom.wordpress.com
nydailynews.com

O

onlyinyourstate.com
opendurham.org
outdoorhub.com

P

pbs.org
planecrashinfo.com
prairieghosts.com
prezi.com

Q

queens.edu

R

raleighnc.gov
ranker.com
realhaunts.com
roadtrippers.com

S

scgenweb.org
sci-news.com
sciway.net
secretary.state.nc.us
704shop.com
sosnc.gov
southeasterntraveler.com
statesville.com
strangeusa.com

T

thecabinet.com
the-dispatch.com
theguardian.com
theshadowlands.net
thirstyworlddesigns.blogspot.com
tripsavvy.com

U

ultimatecampresource.com
unccgdcl.blogspot.com
unexplained-mysteries.com
unknownexplorer.com
urbandictionary.com
usatoday.com

V

visitnc.com

W

wfmynews2.com
wired.com
wral.com
wsoctv.com
www3.gendisasters.co

Y

yourghoststories.com

About the Author

S herman Carmichael, a native of Hemingway, South Carolina, currently lives in Johnsonville, South Carolina. He has been dabbling in things that are best left alone, like ghosts, UFOs, monsters and other strange and unusual things, since he was seventeen years old, and that's a long time. He has seen, heard and felt things that defy explanation. Carmichael's first three books—*Forgotten Tales of South Carolina*, *Legends and Lore of South Carolina* and *Eerie South Carolina*—center on ghosts and the strange and unusual in South Carolina. In his fourth book, *UFOs over South Carolina*, Carmichael takes a closer look at hovering objects and strange lights in the sky. His fifth book, *Strange South Carolina*, returns to the ghostly encounters of South Carolina. Carmichael's sixth book, *Mysterious Tales of Coastal North Carolina*, explores the strange side of coastal North Carolina.

Carmichael has traveled throughout the United States, including Roswell, New Mexico, visiting haunted locations. He has also traveled to Mexico and Central America researching the Mayan ruins. Carmichael plans to continue visiting these unusual places for many years to come. Carmichael worked as a journalist for many years, thirty years as a photographer, thirty years in law enforcement and twelve years in the movie entertainment business.

Visit us at
www.historypress.com